MW00653793

THE SIX-MINUTE MARATHON

A Guide to Life as a Lawyer

THE SIX-MINUTE MARATHON

A Guide to Life as a Lawyer

"Law firms can be very Darwinian; there is constant selective pressure and over time only the fittest associates survive."

Andrew Hartman

Contributing Editor
Caren Ulrich Stacy

NATIONAL INSTITUTE FOR TRIAL ADVOCACY

© 2011 by the National Institute for Trial Advocacy

All rights reserved. No part of this work may be reproduced or transmitted in any form or by any means, electronic or mechanical, including photocopying and recording, or by any information storage or retrieval system without the prior written approval of the National Institute for Trial Advocacy unless such copying is expressly permitted by federal copyright law.

This publication is designed to provide accurate and authoritative information in regard to the subject matter covered. It is sold with the understanding that the author is not engaged in rendering legal services in connection with or as a part of the publication.

The opinions expressed in this publication are solely those of the author and/or the editor and do not necessarily reflect those of the University of Colorado, Cooley LLP or Lawyer Development Strategies LLC. This publication is not endorsed by the University of Colorado, Cooley LLP or Lawyer Development Strategies

Address inquiries to:

Reprint Permission
National Institute for Trial Advocacy
1685 38th Street, Suite 200
Boulder, CO 80301
Phone: (800) 225-6482
Fax: (720) 890-7069
E-mail: permissions@nita.org

Library of Congress Cataloging-in-Publication Data

Hartman, Andrew, 1964-

 The six minute marathon : making the jump from law school to law practice / Andrew Hartman ; contributing editor, Caren Ulrich Stacy.

    p. cm.

"Law firms can be very Darwinian; there is constant selective pressure and over time only the fittest associates survive."

ISBN 978-1-60156-147-3

1. Practice of law--United States. 2. Law--Vocational guidance--United States. 3. Lawyers--Life skills guides. I. Stacy, Caren Ulrich. II. Title.

KF300.H373 2010

340.023'73--dc22

                                2010040699

ISBN 978-1-60156-147-3
FBA 1147
13 12 11 10   10 9 8 7 6 5 4 3 2 1

Printed in the United States of America

To Amy, Jesse & Mica, loves of my life, and thanks Caren!

ACKNOWLEDGMENTS

I had some terrific mentors as an associate. Richard Compere was the best IP litigator I know and a true gentleman. Dan Schlessinger has that rare combination of integrity, intellect, and motivation. Jerry Jacover is a gritty patent litigator not afraid to mess it up. Joel Feldman, the smooth slasher, like a good general, would position his guns to win a case before the first shot was fired at trial.

Along the way, I have also learned from peers, clients, subordinates, and adversaries. John Crittenden has been a great mentor and has reinforced that even partners can (and must) benefit from good counselors. Finally, Amy, an employment lawyer and my wife of twenty plus years; I couldn't have made it without her.

PREFACE

Twenty years of practice, ten years of teaching law school classes and administering an experiential learning program, giving (and receiving) countless associate performance reviews, confirmed for me that law schools struggle to prepare newly minted attorneys for careers in most practices. I decided to write this book to help law students and new lawyers avoid the mistakes I made. I hope the lessons ease your transition from student and junior lawyer to the sometimes Darwinian life of practice.

The Chinese proverb that "a person who enjoys his job never works a day in his life" cannot be more true for the law. I write this book reflecting on many years working in the profession. Some have been stressful and dull, but the vast majority stimulating and fun. Have fun, work with enjoyable colleagues, seek out interesting projects, find balance in your life, be true to yourself, and your days, years, and decades in practice will amount to more than the sum of your paychecks.

Good luck!

Andrew Hartman
Boulder, Colorado

CONTENTS

INTRODUCTION

Over one-third of associates will leave their firm within the first three years, and over three-quarters (77 percent) will be gone within five years.[1] With the uncertain economy and changing law firm environment, we can expect these numbers to become even worse in the years to come. If you are reading this, you are or are about to be a junior associate in private practice or are thinking about a legal career. This book is all about how to succeed and thrive at a moderate- to large-size law firm. The finish line for most lawyers is partnership or a secure alternative offered by the firm. A good friend, born into a Queens, New York, working class Irish Catholic family, who was elected partner at not one but three major national law firms in his twenty-five year career, offers any associate who will listen this advice:

> *Making partner at a big firm is like winning a pie*
> *eating contest where the prize is more pie.*

It is important to bear in mind that making partner or an equivalent position will not fundamentally change your practice. You will gain some benefits, some degree of security, but with it a lot more responsibility. If you are unhappy as an associate, however, you will not be happy if promoted. If you are miserable, get out when you can! The pie eating comment is the most accurate statement about promotion I have ever heard—keep it close.

Partnership is the brass ring because for lawyers in private practice, partnership is typically the best long-term option.

---

1. Janet Ellen Raasch, *Making Partner—Or Not: Is It In, Up or Over in the 21st Century?*, ABA Law Practice Magazine, June 2007, v. 33 No. 4 at 32.

These days many firms are now offering meaningful alternatives to partnership. Throughout this book the term "partnership" will also include these alternatives that offer a secure and meaningful practice.

Partnership, in its many forms, is very hard to achieve and no one teaches you how. Libraries are filled with self-help books on succeeding in business, in sales, in school, even in law school, but there is nary a tome on how to make it once you are here. There are a few gripe books out there by disgruntled associates and books by outsiders looking in, but not from an insider who was been through the wringer and survived.

What follows are tips on how to extend your reach for your best chance to grasp that brass ring of partnership and promotion at your firm. I have been fortunate to have experienced a path of success (having made mistakes along the way) and want to help you with your travels—help I never had and most never receive. Some of the items in this book may seem petty compared with what you learned in law school and what you believe makes a good lawyer. Let's face it, the business world can be petty, and since it is usually easy to traverse trivial issues, better know the rules of the game so your best qualities shine through.

New lawyers usually do not have in-depth experience working at a sizable law firm; this book can help. Inexperienced lawyers make the same mistakes over and over because, well, they are inexperienced. It would be nice to debate and discuss the shortfalls of today's legal education, but, while interesting, law schools will not change dramatically anytime soon. I have banged my head against the ivy covered walls of law schools from the outside and am now trying to effectuate some change from within. Change will come, but it will be on a slow boat.

Almost every practicing lawyer will tell you that law school does not really prepare lawyers for practice. Law school classes do a very good job in helping pupils think and reason, but beyond that, students are mostly on their own. The closest opportunities to practice while in law school are clinical programs and externships. Some law firms take meaningful steps to mentor and educate associates. My old shop Cooley, for instance, has Cooley College, which is the model for most in-house associate education programs. Associates must attend a week or so of training during their first year with follow-up courses as they advance. Even firms that excel at skill development for associates still do not, and cannot, provide young attorneys with all the tools they need to make it to the finish line. NITA, my dear publisher, also offers a suite of courses for lawyers at all levels on various important development topics.

I had been in private practice since 1989 after graduating from Georgetown. I have been a partner at a large and profitable technology-oriented national law firm where I was the head of the junior associate evaluation process. Also, I have taught as an adjunct law professor at the University of Colorado since 2001, supervised independent study students, and coached moot court teams. Now I am on the inside trying to help the academy with experiential education. These positions have convinced me of the need to write a book to help fill the gaps in legal education and law firm mentoring.

Law school is not vocational education—freshly minted lawyers are not prepared to practice right out of the box. Law school is not a trade school nor should it be. But law schools do fail to teach students about some basic legal practices. My bright and hard-working law students usually do not know even how to write a simple business letter. Firms' summer associates and junior attorneys do not know how to keep time sheets—the bread and butter of law firm economics. Associates generally do not know how big firms operate. For me, since law school in the '80s and for years later, I was a total babe in the woods. Luckily, there were some great mentors along the way. Even with help, I made many mistakes. This book can hopefully assist you in avoiding some of those same mistakes.

You will often hear that private practice is a marathon, not a sprint—but you record that race six minutes at a time. To bill two thousand hours a year, an associate must account for 120,000 billable minutes. Over the ten year or so partnership tract at major firms, this amounts to over a million minutes of billable time. It is no wonder the statistics show that associate burnout at large firms is a major problem. Consider how few lawyers are promoted to partner at big firms and how many lawyers hang up their gloves *completely* after a few years, leaving the practice entirely. Much of this can be attributed to a disconnect between education, skills training, and expectations. I am not saying that this book can make you partner or get you promoted, but it can help you along the way, like a good mentor, and make the million minutes a little easier.

Learning the practice is a lifelong endeavor; you will not feel settled for a decade or more. This book will give you some essential components of a large firm practice that you did not learn in school and that most successful lawyers had to pick up along the way.

But don't just take it from me. My contributing editor, and reality checker, Caren Ulrich Stacy, is an accomplished fifteen-plus-year veteran of large national and international law firms. She has worked with some of the most reputable and respected law firms in the country, including Arnold & Porter LLP, Cooley, McGuireWoods, Weil Gotshal & Manges LLP, and Jenkens & Gilchrist. During her tenure at these firms, she has contributed to the hiring, development, and advancement of over 3,500 lawyers. Caren has also helped outplace those who didn't make it. She is clearly an authority on survival and success in law firms. You will see notes from her throughout the book—pay attention. Together, we hope to guide you through the unique world of practice in BigLaw by learning from the mistakes of those who came before you. The rest is up to you. We wish you luck and Godspeed.

CHAPTER 1

THAT AIN'T WORKIN'—INTERVIEWS AND OFFERS

Before we jump into the practice of law, let's review some job interview basics for those who are still in school, may not have a job lined up, or may be in the market for a new position. Most law school career services departments actually do very well at preparing students for interviews. The placement administrators are usually in touch with the outside world and may even have been employed by a law firm in the past decade.

Students who reviewed this book commented that it is fine to prepare me for work, but how do I get a job in the first place? This is too big a topic to tackle in one chapter, or even one book. We suggest that your school's career services office is the first place to start. The placement officers are typically very skilled at counseling and helping you develop an effective plan. Almost all law schools will have services available for alumni, as well as current students. This is a resource that your tuition pays, and law school deans want you to succeed in the job search since well employed law students lead to better school ranking, increased giving, and important professional outreach.

The first rule about interviewing is to know yourself, your school, and the firm. Big law firms are very selective; grades and credentials are thoroughly examined. If you are on law review or have other stellar academic credentials, you will have more opportunities than others. If you are at a top tier school, you will have more choices. However, if you have lower grades, you will need to make up ground. By the time you interview, it may be too late to do much about grades and you cannot change the school's reputation. Therefore, you will need to show desirable nonacademic attributes such as moot court competitions, real-life experience (e.g., corporate jobs, engineering, accounting), judicial externships, publications, community/national service, and the like.

Caren's Advice

And if you have not done so already, participate in mock interviews at your law school. Having coordinated and participated in over 7,000 on-campus and callback interviews, I have seen the #1 law student at a top 50 school not get one single offer, and many less credentialed law students get numerous offers as a result of their interviewing abilities.

In addition, I suggest you note experiences that separate you from your peers, e.g., professional or NCAA sports, public performance or musical talent, military service, language skills, leadership roles, overcoming adversity; even being an Eagle Scout can open doors. One of my law partners still lists Eagle Scout on his biography because the outside world views it as a major accomplishment and an insight into his character although he is over fifty and hasn't been involved in scouting for many decades.

Think about what attributes separate you from the crowd in a positive way and highlight them.

Caren's Advice

Rely on more than just your resume to market your best qualities. Use social networking sites such as LinkedIn, Facebook, and Twitter to elaborate on and highlight important successes or leaderships abilities. If you were captain of the debate team, list some of your big wins on LinkedIn. Or if you chaired a volunteer effort to raise money for a nonprofit organization, show pictures of the positive outcomes on Facebook. But do note, there is a flip side to this as well. If you have entries or pictures on your sites that do not portray a professional demeanor (think beer bong), consider removing them while you are interviewing. Law firms typically review your online presence as part of the recruitment process.

Even if you have great grades, you still need self-examination. What is your personality, how do you present, are you a confident person, are you shy, are you charismatic, are you bookish, sporty, nerdy, dynamic? You need to know yourself so you can present an appropriate image to employers. Speak with someone you can trust and try to obtain an honest assessment, or you may be in for an unfortunate surprise. If you had job performance reviews in the past, remember the comments and try to understand yourself. You will always need to be true to yourself, and knowledge about how others perceive you is crucial.

Let me digress for a moment on people who will try to separate you from your money—playing on your fear and uncertainty. Although some may add value as you develop in business, I would not recommend career coaches at this stage. Most of these folks will not be of benefit to junior lawyers in private practice because they (1) are likely less familiar with how law firms operate than your school's placement office or (2) their skills may not be suited for recent graduates or students, but are more focused on established professionals. Career, or executive, coaches can charge an awful lot and may not add materially to your job hunt. Instead, rely on your school's placement and other resources—research and your social network. You have made it this far and should be able to line up a great position.

Another person you may not need right now is the resume consultant. Résumés are pretty straightforward documents, and you will find countless free samples on the Web or at the law school's career office. Unless you are a late entry into the law field, keep your resume at one page, highlighting academics, job experiences, and credentials that set you apart. That should be sufficient in most cases. As with career consultants, in most situations if you are confident in yourself and utilize free resources, your resume and related documents will be powerful.

Caren's Advice

Andy is correct—there is no need to pay anyone to review your resume. But do have someone review it carefully as a second (and maybe even third) pair of eyes. Mistakes on your resume are fatal. I once worked with a hiring partner at a major NY law firm who would automatically file resumes with spelling errors in the "no" category regardless of the law student's credentials.

Your resume and interviews should highlight why you are a great applicant. The ideal big firm associate candidate is someone with outstanding credentials, relevant experience, confidence, an outgoing personality, and a presentable disposition.

Caren's Advice

Why is this the ideal candidate you ask? Because this is the type of person who often appeals to clients. Note that everything done in law firms is done with the client's needs and satisfaction in mind.

However, hardly anyone has the complete package. If you are shy, you will need to make an extra effort to ask questions and avoid uncomfortable silences during interviews. Even if it is against your nature, you will have to buy decent clothes and know how to wear them. If your grades are not great but you have other attributes, you need to highlight those.

If you are not at a top school, but have a *positive* reason for being where you are (not simply that you partied through undergrad), make sure prospective employers know this. Perhaps you are at the second-tier school because of a full academic scholarship, proximity to family or employment, or the school may have a particular specialty that you desire. Have at your ready for the interviewer good, positive reasons for why you are at a lower ranked school. The law school rating "system" is not without controversy, so poking a hole or two in it can help in your search.

Apart from knowing yourself and where your school plays, it is important to research the firms on your interview list. How do you gather information on law firms? There is no substitute for research, so don't look for quick fixes.

Research sources are multiple—firm Web sites, media, other lawyers or students, Internet, guidebooks, blogs, chat rooms. The key is to gather a lot of information and then *make your own judgment* about the firm since there is so much unreliable data. Most misinformation comes from unreliable sources—blogs, chat rooms, etc.—but there can also be poor material from sources that look credible. Be critical. Don't take the *Insider's Guide* or any single source as gospel. Some information is reliable, some not.

You are blessed and cursed to be practicing during the information age. The key is to translate the information into knowledge. When I attended law school in the '80s, there was a code of secrecy within and among law firms. There was little or no disclosure of information. This was pre-Internet, pre-GreedyAssociates.com, pre-FindLaw.com, pre-abovethelaw. com. Law students and associates were almost completely in the dark.

One of the amusing and early sources of knowledge, of choppy utility however, was an "underground" newsletter called, *The Rodent: The Official Underground Publication for Law Firm Associates*. More on the *Rodent* later. You need reliable information to help with the interview and beyond.

The law firm interviewer will probably be a mid-level associate or young partner. She will look for credentials, of course, but also for how you "fit" with the firm. Thus, you need to know something about the firm and why you are interested in the particular position. Also, you should have a geographic link to the office. If you have no obvious geographic ties, you need to come up with something credible, like you've *always* wanted to practice law in Hawaii.

One trick to get in the door with a national firm is to select an office where there are the most openings and opportunities even if it is not your top geographic choice. Once you are at the firm, there is greater chance to transfer to another office. Some offices need more associates because they are in vibrant economic zones or because they are in a tough-sell city. If you can gut it out for a couple years, there is a chance to transfer intra-firm, and you will have bolstered your resume. You may also be able to parlay a summer clerkship offer from a less desirable office to a more interesting one after you have impressed the firm. Your career will be long and a brief stint in a second choice geography could cement a top position where you want to live long term. Be flexible.

Another reason to be geographically flexible is that the reputation of law schools varies greatly based on location. While Harvard, Stanford, and Michigan have stellar national reputations, Colorado is very strong in Denver and the mountain west, but fades as you travel east. Selecting a regional office that plays to your school's strength increases the chance of success for callbacks and offers.

You should receive a callback if the interviewer likes you, there is an opening, and you meet whatever minimum academic standards the firm has defined.

How do you pass the first hurdle, the one you can control most at the interview? Your law school career services office will help you with some good questions to ask interviewers. If you are shy, role playing interviews with friends can help. Season your resume with items that would appeal to employers and that might introduce interesting discussions, such as sports, performance arts, etc. If the thirty minute on campus interview flies by, and you have friendly banter with the attorney, that is a good sign. If there are awkward silences and you don't seem to connect, that is bad. If this happens, make changes for the next interview. Again, be flexible and use each interview as a learning experience.

If you can find the name of the interviewer in advance, research her background on Martindale-Hubble or the firm's Web site. There is a good chance your school's placement office will know the names of those coming to campus, so inquire. You can also call the firm's recruiting coordinator and ask who the firm is sending.

Make sure not to overdo attempts at making connections with interviewers, you could seem obsequious, which no one likes.

Also, I suggest avoiding any gimmicks like bringing props to the interview or sending gifts to the attorney. You will make an impression, but not a good one. Most hiring attorneys say that gimmicks don't work, strong interviewing skills do.

Interviewing skills are tough to teach, but I have some suggestions for ways to avoid obvious pitfalls. Steer clear of controversial subjects, such as politics, in discussions and on your resume. Don't always say what's on your mind. Even if the interview appears casual, it is not. Here's a true story: a male law student had an interview with a female associate. The associate was a pleasant and casual person. She asked what the student's classmates were like. He said, "I like most of them, but I think some of the women are here to get that M-R-S degree that they missed back in undergrad." I certainly couldn't make up something like that. Would he get a callback?

The interview is NOT the time to assert your independence; don't think, "If they don't like me for what I am, I don't want to work there." After receiving multiple job offers you can make that decision from a position of strength. Until then, first impressions matter. Be prepared to discuss everything on your resume, and things that are not. Have at least three good questions in hand, such as: (1) Where do you see your (the firm's) practice in five years? (2) What made you choose this firm? and (3) What's the most interesting matter you worked on in the last year? Hint—they can be the same three for every interview. Be prepared to answer obvious questions (e.g., Why do you want to work here? Why did you go to law school? What is your favorite class?).

> ### Caren's Advice
>
> OK, now what questions NOT to ask during the interview as well. For instance, it is not a good time to ask if part-time is an option for junior associates during OCI (on campus interviewing). You may have an excellent reason for wanting to know, but wait until you have an offer to ask. To some interviewers that question may signal that you don't want to work very hard your first year.

While seemingly the least important, dress for success. A senior associate at a large, ultra-conservative Wall Street firm rejected a candidate because he wore rubber-soled penny loafers to an interview. Reasoning: if the candidate wasn't perceptive enough to wear classic, lace-up, leather-soled business shoes, he would not make it with the firm's conservative culture. Irrational? Maybe. But there is actually some logic. When the firm needs to decide who to call back among the dozens of thirty-minute interviewees, the interviewer makes countless snap decisions. There was something about wearing the casual shoes that signaled that the student would not fit it.

An interesting paradox in interviews is that while law firms are very selective, all on-campus interviewers want to succeed in calling back quality candidates. They *want* to invite a few good men and women to the next phase. The interviewing attorneys typically visit your school because they are alumni or have some interest in being there. Therefore not calling anyone back is seen as a personal failure. Landing a star is a personal victory. You are thus not only measured against the firm's criteria, but you are also compared to your peers who are interviewing that day. Make sure you are the star that is called back.

The callback interview is basically the same as on campus, but there are more opportunities to shine or to blow it. You will have more time to research the firm and hone your interest. Use the firm's recruiting coordinator as an ally for information—there is no need to feel your way in the dark. Almost every recruiting director is a people person, eager to help out. His or her job is to help the firm *hire* associates, not reject them. The recruiting director will usually be the firm's point person facilitating your visit.

Caren's Advice

Do remember, however, that you are not the only recruit. There are hundreds of students interviewing with the firm during this time period. You should call the recruiter with critical questions, but don't put her on your speed dial. She or someone at the firm will undoubtedly make contact with you when necessary. It often comes up during hiring meetings and can affect offer decisions if a candidate is not using good judgment during the interview process—such as calling the recruiter incessantly.

You might be flown in and put up at a fancy hotel. This might be a new experience for you. Use some common sense with travel costs and reimbursements—don't be a pig or make rookie mistakes. Submitting a huge dinner tab or trashing your hotel room will not win any points.

Here is a fun story that actually happened to one of my former colleagues: a small town gal from central Illinois attended the University of Illinois, which was located near her rural hometown, for undergrad and law school. Let's call her Olive. Olive was one of those people who rarely left her county of birth. She had only been to Chicago a few times and never stayed at a fancy hotel. She never traveled to any other big cities. A prestigious, liberal law firm that was Olive's first choice called her back for interviews in Chicago and put her up at a fancy new downtown hotel—the Four Seasons on Michigan Avenue. The interviews went great, and Olive was very excited. She even returned to school with gifts from Chicago for all her buddies—tiny bottles of top shelf booze and fancy nuts.

"The firm was so great," Olive said earnestly, "The hotel even stocked this little dorm fridge with drinks and snacks for me. I couldn't drink much in Chicago and didn't want it to go to waste."

Olive's worldlier, and clearly mortified, friends explained the foreign concept of a hotel minibar, and the $500 tab she just incurred. The poor student immediately was on the phone with the firm's recruiting coordinator. Olive got the offer and everyone at the firm joked about the story for years. The main reason Olive earned a job offer—aside from her talents—was that she fessed up right away instead of waiting until the hotel served the law firm with a huge bar bill. This showed character, maturity, and judgment, with some innocent naiveté rather than boorishness.

Another tip for the call back: if you can swing it, try to say hello to your on-campus interviewer. You obviously made a good impression on her. Ask the recruiting coordinator if this is possible and follow up with one of the attorneys you see that day. You probably want to drop the person a short e-mail thanking her for the callback and saying what day you will be in. If you really clicked with the on-campus attorney, reinforcing the connection can only help you get the offer since she is likely on the hiring committee.

I hope that your interviews go well and that you have many offers of employment from which to choose. Then how do you decide which firm's offer to accept? The first rule is that law students, including your know-it-all friends, don't know diddly about law firms. Admit that and you can avoid painful mistakes. The second rule is that law firms, like law students, accentuate the positive and minimize the negative. In another words, don't get suckered with a bait and switch or you will end up with a Yugo when you wanted a Mercedes-Benz.

How do you check behind the veil? There are many publications that can give you a peek under the hood at major law firms. *The Insider's Guide*, abovethelaw.com, and Internet chat rooms can be helpful for data mining, but take what they say about the firms with a whole heap of salt. Most young associates who post on chat rooms and provide data for surveys actually don't know much either, have an ax to grind, or are plants, shilling for the firm.

Caren's Advice

Check out the firm's rankings on the Vault and American Lawyer surveys too. Your school's placement office will have access to these surveys and you can find them online. But, as Andy mentioned, be careful not to put too much stock in the results. Many of the survey results are not representative samplings of the associate population. If only 5 percent of the associates completed the survey, you cannot be sure that the perceived issues are widespread. That said, do ask about issues raised in the surveys that concern you. And ask more than one person to see if you get the same answers consistently.

Unfortunately, many firms hide important facts. Here are some issues to ponder: does the firm specialize in low billing commodity work, like some insurance defense firms, or does it have marquis corporate clients? Is there a culture of partner co-operation and collegiality or is the firm compensation "eat what you kill"? Is the leadership democratically selected by competitive election or is it nominated in a self-perpetuating politburo style? Is pro bono really valued? Does the firm seem organized, efficient, and well run? Are the partners dynamic and energetic, or staid and stodgy? Do the associates seem happy to be there or are they just punching the clock? Is there a lot of attorney turnover? Even this short list of items is hard to decipher, so there is a simple test.

If you have many job choices, one of the best litmus tests of the firm is to review the credentials of the associates and partners. These are available on the firms' Web sites. The rule is basic: the best firms attract and retain or were founded by the most qualified lawyers. If the firm claims first-class status but is populated by less than highly credentialed lawyers, there is a problem. Pretend you are a potential client interviewing the associates and partners. Did they attend top notch schools? Do they have academic honors, judicial clerkships, big time litigation or deal experience? The practice of law is a meritocracy with the best lawyers joining the best firms attracting the best work.

If you have a choice of positions, make it based on hard facts as well as whether you enjoyed the people you met during the interviews. After you choose, you will be thrown into the real business world. The next chapters will help you along the way. If you are still in the job hunt, don't despair. Persistence and a positive attitude will be your best assets.

Chapter 2

Give 'Em What They Want— Managing Managers

What do partners and senior associates want from summer associates and new hires? There is obviously more than one answer, and the target is often frustratingly in motion. The primary characteristic that senior attorneys expect, demand, and require in successful junior associates and summers is the ability to instill confidence that the job at hand will be done, done well, done on time, and done completely. This is sometimes called the "sleep-at-night test."

A new associate passes this test if the senior lawyer can leave the office (probably hours before the associate) and not stare at the ceiling all night fearing that things will blow up. The sleep-at-night test demands that associates counsel clients without constant supervision, research and write documents on their own, and practice with professionalism. The associates need to produce quality work, not just bill large quantities of time.

Why aren't long hours enough? Working hard may be easy to grasp, but long hours are not the be all, end all of law firm needs. Some of the top rated, most respected associates at big law firms are not the ones with the highest billable hour totals—it takes more. In fact, if an associate consistently bills extremely high hours without achieving results, his productivity actually becomes suspect; the strong billables become a negative. Compare this to a steady biller who produces quality work and meets the sleep-at-night test.

Caren's Advice

It takes deliberate practice and training to become an exceptional legal practitioner. Studies confirm that having "talent" is not always enough. Take every advantage of the training opportunities and resources offered by the firm. In your first few years, say yes whenever possible (without overextending yourself) to commercial and pro bono work that affords you new and varying experiences. You may have to work more hours than your counterparts during the first few years, but you will also gain more skills and experience.

As associates progress at the firm, there will be other important requirements like complex skill development, business generation, leadership, and practice management. Right now, let's stick with the basics—the sleep-at-night test. The tricky business is that different managers require different skills to pass the test. A mantra in this book is that you need to know your audience—what works splendidly with someone may fail miserably with another. There are, however, some common elements that every partner and senior associate will demand.

Caren's Advice

Do your research. Find one or two mid-senior associates who have worked for the partner previously. Ask them about his style, pet peeves, and quirks.

Partners and senior associates will expect you to be responsive; take notes when given an assignment; ask probing questions; show attentiveness, energy, and enthusiasm; hop to it; give progress reports (the amount here is the big variable); and present *completed* projects on a timely basis. Managers refuse to hear that you don't have time for the assignment, that you can't meet a deadline, or that you can't produce a complete project. None of this means you act without direction, however.

Caren's Advice

Take the initiative to learn about the BIG PICTURE. Understanding the client's end goal and the overall case strategy will be immeasurably valuable as you work on your narrow portion of the project. Learn about the client's business and become familiar with important case materials. The firm may provide billable credit for these activities, but don't expect it. Think of the time as an investment in your career and the possibility to take on a bigger role with the case or client in the future.

If you seem to be flailing with a problem, ask for help. There are two theories on asking for help: Concentrate all your questions on one person. While he may think you're a complete idiot, everyone else thinks you're a genius. Or spread the questions around, causing a little hesitation in everyone, but not tipping off any one person. It's really your choice, but do not hesitate to ask questions. Sometimes asking the wrong question can be painful, though, so be careful.

While it is appropriate to ask for help, technology has advanced such that the wrong "all hands" e-mail can make you look like a complete dolt. For example, a new litigation associate with solid academic credentials sent an e-mail around inquiring about the most basic question of law; years later, attorneys still remark about that e-mail.

A Harvard-educated associate asked about how a client could circumvent a court order. That resulted in firm-wide discussions about his lack of acumen and judgment. To make matters worse, he later sent around another all hands e-mail saying that he had found the answer. Do tell. He really meant to ask about appellate review, mandamus, or reconsideration of a court order, and whether the original ruling could be stayed pending the review. As one of his fellow associates mentioned at the time, "Take away the shovel, he's hit bedrock." That one e-mail eroded the presumption of confidence given to a highly credentialed junior lawyer. Clear communication is crucial to success, and it is often difficult to be clear in e-mail. Before sending any e-mail, give it a second read to make certain it is unambiguous.

Caren's Advice

Another potentially fatal e-mail mistake is "replying to all" to an all hands e-mail. Just assume it is never OK to reply to all. You may be the wittiest associate on the block, but now is not your time to shine.

How do you instill confidence in senior attorneys that allows you to achieve independence and success? After years of receiving and then giving associate reviews, and as past chairperson of a major law firm's junior associate review committee, I find that several themes are repeatedly attached to quality associates:

- assuredness and confidence
- responsiveness
- ability to act independently
- strong communication skills

Caren's Advice

This includes grammar and spelling. Elementary mistakes often signal red flags to the partners that there are bigger issues with the associate's work product. Check, double check, and get a second pair of eyes on all of your documents. If your secretary is not a great proofreader, find a go-to in document processing.

- success as a team player, yet always accountable
- leadership

- willingness to put in hours when needed
- dedication to the practice, clients, and the firm
- intelligence
- judgment
- discretion
- orientation toward service
- positive can-do attitude
- insight
- creativity
- good relations with peers, staff, and subordinates
- rapid skill development
- maturity beyond his experience

Caren's Advice

There is one other essential attribute that combines some of those Andy mentioned—initiative. Every partner I know mentions this trait as critical when reflecting on the most effective associates. Partners love associates who take ownership of their work and provide suggestions on next steps when possible. Don't just do your portion of the project and then retreat to your office to await your next project. Instead, hand in the project, ask for feedback on what you have done so far, and then suggest how you might be able to help with the case going forward.

Associates perceived as middling, workaday lawyers lack many of these positive attributes. While it is rare that an associate is truly unintelligent or lazy—the hiring process weeds out most of those—typical problems of associates are ones of perception that most can easily correct.

A side note about summer associate positions. All of the rules in this book apply to summer associates as well as permanent associates. The summer program is an extended interview where you are evaluated as if you were an associate. Of course, summer programs are more fun and have lower billing expectations, but you still need to take the work seriously and produce excellent results.

The summer program is proving ground for whether a law student can cut it as a full-time associate. Likewise, junior associates are expected to grow the skills needed to develop into senior associates. Finally, senior associates must meet partnership, or similar, expectations in order to gain promotion. Failure to recognize what is expected of you is the biggest error an associate can make. You must be aware, alert, and responsive. Here's how.

CHAPTER 3

FIRST DAY OF MY LIFE—HOW TO MAKE IT GOOD

Law firms can be very Darwinian; there is constant selective pressure and over time only the fittest associates survive. This is true even with "lifestyle" firms, firms that profess not to be cutthroat. Partners at most top firms are the best and brightest (or think they are) and want associates who have the same abilities. What you do right out of the box will have a big impact on your career.

It's the first day of work. You have survived law school, interviews, and the bar exam. (You haven't passed yet, so that's still a worry, and there will always be some smart aleck who reminds you that no one has ever failed the bar exam at the firm and you don't want to be the first, blah, blah, blah. The same joker may tell you that many famous lawyers, John F. Kennedy Jr., Mayor Richard M. Daley, failed on their first bar tries. They will say it as a joke, but you will still worry a little, and you probably don't have a famous lineage to pull you past the finish line.) If you are a summer associate, you have completed the toughest two years of class work and can now prove yourself in the real or pseudo-real world.

The first thing full-time associates must know, in case you haven't heard, *practicing law for real is not like the firm's summer program*. Let me repeat that *practicing law for real is not like the firm's summer program.* Your first day or two may be as close as you will ever come to that fun-filled, carefree summer. You can start on the right foot with some good planning.

Most big firms will hire you to be either a corporate lawyer or a litigator. While some firms hire into specialties, like tax or intellectual property, most associates will float around for a while before they have to "declare a major." Assuming you are not slotted into a particular practice, you should determine what areas of the law interest you and research who at the firm engages in that type of work.

For instance, if you are a corporate associate interested in venture capital financing hired into the general corporate department, determine which partners and associates have a VC practice. You then can gravitate towards them, learn the ropes, and develop a specialty in the years to come. If you do not educate yourself and take control of assignments, you will be stuck with whatever projects come along—usually the dogs—since other, more alert, associates will snatch the plums.

Although you are a junior associate and low person on the totem pole, that does not mean you have to relinquish control of your career. Start by researching the firm's attorney biographies. Who is interesting? If you were in the summer program, you have a great advantage since you already know practice groups and personalities. If you did not have this benefit, network within the firm, as discussed in detail below, to gain the knowledge you need to find interesting projects. Same is true, but to a lesser extent, for summer associates since you will likely be forced into a broader experience. Even so, you can still take control of the situation. A great way to gain control is through internal networking.

Caren's Advice

Learn about the firm's work assignment process. Are projects handed out by specific "assignment brokers" or is it a free-market system? Either way, learn the process and make it work to your benefit. If you are expected to get your projects through a broker, make sure she is familiar with the type of work you want to do and with whom. If it is a free-market system, also known as survival of the fittest, be proactive. Seek out the partners with whom you want to work and approach them directly. Whatever the scenarios, do not, and I repeat, do not leave it up to the luck of the draw. You are responsible for your career. The firm will provide developmental resources to help you succeed, but it is ultimately up to you to take advantage of the opportunities.

Internal networking, what does that mean? First off, do you have a friend from the summer program, law school, or college who can be a guide at the firm? A guide can be invaluable. If you come up blank, check the attorney bios and see who shares your background. Don't just look at schooling, however, when seeking out a guide and potential mentor or confidant.

Many experiences actually engender greater loyalty than college or law school. Did you serve in the armed forces? Find a fellow vet and gain an immediate friend and ally. Social fraternities are also fertile ground. Where did your colleagues grow up? Shared upbringing, even separated by a decade, can provide a comforting link. Think of this as networking with your colleagues—a theme that I will raise often in this book.

When you find your mentor or guide, hopefully *before* your first day, ask the hard questions. If you have chosen well, she will be happy to share. Who is interesting to work with? Who makes unreasonable demands? Who is loyal and who is a backstabber? Who has power? Where is the power?

> ## Caren's Advice
>
> In addition to proactively seeking out guides as Andy suggested, take advantage of formal programs within your firm. Most firms have mentoring programs in which they pair new associates with more experienced lawyers. They say it takes a village to raise a child. The same is true for lawyers. You will, and should, have numerous mentors throughout your career who will guide you on different aspects of the practice. You might have one mentor who helps to guide your career, one who offers specialty or niche advice, and another who teaches you about client relations. Listen and learn—these mentors will be your best allies and champions as you strive for partnership.

Mentors can help you figure out power centers in the firm. Power is an interesting thing in law firms, however. Sometimes it lies where you don't expect to find it, and sometimes the managing partner, someone you would think powerful, is a mere figurehead. Therefore, don't simply look at partners as power centers.

Other associates, paralegals, and even staff can have significant power; they can assist or impede your advancement, but more on that in the teamwork section that follows.

An example of hidden power comes from my old Chicago firm, which had a very active federal litigation practice. We had two docket clerks who were in charge of courthouse filings, docketing dates into a central calendar system, and general litigation nuts and bolts (this was pre-electronic filing). In addition to being amazing fonts of information on civil practice and procedure, they were very influential in firm matters and could actually advance or retard associates' development. A good word to a partner could boost an associate's career. Fortunately, they were both good natured, and you had to be a real jerk to garner their ire.

At Cooley's Colorado office, the longest serving professional is a paralegal specialist. In addition to being a great practitioner, she worked elbow to elbow with most of the firm's leadership since they were tots, or a least junior associates. When you have history, and know where the bodies are buried, you gain a lot of influence even if you are "just" a paralegal.

It is also crucial to gather information on major firm clients and referral sources since they also have power and influence over your development. Except in certain plaintiffs' class-action work, clients are the lifeblood of large firms. If you can work with important firm clients, and kick butt, your stature will rise. Find out who the firm's main clients are. Often, there may be a very diffuse client base, but only a few key referral sources. This is the case in insurance defense, venture capital work, or other highly specialized practices. Find out who the clients are, who controls the flow of work, and use the information to get on the A team.

One of Cooley's former corporate partners (and my current law partner) is an avid bicyclist. When taking an early morning ride years ago as a senior associate, he wiped out and ended up in the ER, scraped and bloody. The associate had the presence of mind to remember a 9:00 a.m. meeting with the CFO of the office's largest referral source. He left a voice mail from the hospital asking to reschedule the meeting. The CFO was so taken with the sense of responsibility that he e-mailed the message in a wave file to all the corporate partners at the firm. Needless to say, this message from a powerful referral source circulated around the partnership and aided the associate's reputation for responsibility and client service.

Before you start work you should have learned a lot about the firm's lawyers, clients, practices, and power structure. You have thought about areas of practice that you want to pursue. The next step is to act on this knowledge.

Your first day will be filled with paperwork, training, and introductions. It is common for someone to show you around the office to meet your colleagues. This is a good time to tell that venture capital partner or associate that you are *really* interested in her practice and that you'd love to help out. Everyone likes a little flattery and someone taking an interest in their work. Try to remember a few key transactions or cases and mention them without appearing unctuous. If you don't have a chance to see someone during the routine tour, tell your guide that you would like to meet a particular person or simply knock on the door and introduce yourself. This will pay dividends.

With good planning and proactiveness, you will seek and receive projects that interest you. Do a good job, and you will become the go-to associate on those projects. Although you want interesting assignments, you should almost never turn away work when you are just starting. First impressions are everything, and now is the time to market yourself to the firm.

Caren's Advice

Unless of course you can't deliver. Juggling projects will be one of your biggest challenges as a new associate. Ask for guidance from the assigning partners when trying to prioritize your workload.

There are many opportunities to market yourself. One of my friends just starting out at the firm was told by a jaded senior associate to avoid working for a particular partner because he was rather odd, not evil, just different. Because of this reputation, the partner had trouble finding associates to help with his practice. My friend, a bit hesitantly, offered to help. They hit it off and a very positive professional relationship blossomed. Years later, when the partner was ready to slow down his practice, he handed many important client relations to his key associate, helping the associate become a major rainmaker at a critical time in his career.

This story is an example of a marketing theme you will hear throughout this book—in the beginning of your career, the most important clients are your own colleagues.

Caren's Advice

This point is so important that it warrants repeating. The senior associates and partners with whom you work are your clients. Treat them exactly as you would the in-house counsel at the firm's largest client. Write e-mails, draft documents, and manage time with that mantra in mind.

Later, you will gain actual client responsibility and things will change, but it is always important to keep your internal marketing sharp. Most successful partners will tell you that even with a huge book of business, it is your *partners* who deserve and require prompt attention.

Caren's Advice

Caren's Advice: Internal networking should be a major part of your marketing efforts as a junior lawyer. Attend the rubber-chicken dinner banquets where your firm has purchased a table and sit next to the senior partners. Go to every happy hour event in the office to mingle with lawyers in other practice areas. Attend training sessions to get to know other lawyers at your same experience level. The more lawyers youknow, the better equipped you will be to find the resources you need and get the best assignments early in your career.

For those who were in the summer program, the firm will know you, and you have probably already done a good job with internal marketing. If you are new to the firm, it is very important to recognize how you are perceived. First impressions are very important. Here are some ways to make the best impression you can.

CHAPTER 4

MY FRIENDS ALL DRIVE PORSCHES— FAST CARS, NATTY CLOTHES, AND THE GOOD LIFE

You are brilliant, well educated, motivated, talented, ambitious, hard working, dedicated, and loyal. You wear clothes from college, own one cheap suit, a pair of old shoes, and drive your grandfather's Buick Skylark. Which do your new colleagues see first? Your dedication or your image? Your talents or your grandpa's beater? If ninety percent of life is just showing up, the other ten percent may be how you look after showing up.

Clothing may not really make the man or woman, but the wrong attire can kill your confidence and make a poor start to your career. Your vast collection of worn jeans and concert tee shirts will have limited value in the business world, and, like it or not, you will need to go shopping. Wearing appropriate, clean, well fitting, and quality attire will give you confidence and can help make a good first impression.

What do you wear the first day and beyond? The simple answer is that you should wear the *type*, but not necessarily the *style*, of clothing that others don at your firm. This is another time where forward recon is crucial. You will feel and look silly if you sport jeans and everyone else wears dark suits. Vice versa of course. By now, most firms have adopted some form of business casual, but many practices still require classic business clothes, suits for men, professional combos or conservative dresses for women. In particular, active litigation practices, banking practices, regulatory, and probate practices typically will require formal business attire. The probate attorneys I know say that they have to be ready to attend a funeral at a moment's notice. Business casual is not what you wear to clean the garage; look at successful attorneys you know and find a style that fits.

> ## Caren's Advice
>
> It is also important to pay attention to what your clients are wearing. I worked for a large tech-based law practice in Silicon Valley during the boom in the early 2000s. Lawyers were still wearing suits at that point, while most of their clients were wearing Bermuda shorts and flip-flops. One of the clients sent a nice, but clearly intentioned e-mail to the partners asking that they wear more casual clothing when visiting the client's office because "all of the suits were scaring the engineers and programmers."

An important clothes tip: hang an extra set of traditional business attire, an outfit complete with shoes and accessories, on the back of your office door, especially if your firm is business casual most of the time. You may have to run to court unexpectedly or attend a formal meeting. It would be a shame to lose a great opportunity because you weren't dressed properly for a conference or hearing. Having a set of clothes hanging on the back of your office door also gives the *appearance* that you are ready for anything—it instills confidence.

One mistake attorneys make in doing this is that they enlist a second- or third-string outfit for the job. Ironically, if you need to grab this outfit, it is probably for something really important. Because you want to look and feel your best, hang a decent suit and check it periodically for style and size.

Caren's Advice

This will probably come across as sexist, but some old habits die hard in the legal industry. Ladies: wear skirt-suits, not pant-suits to court. There are judges, and even juries, who live in the dark ages. They will reprimand you, sometimes openly, for not adhering to the same old-fashioned rules they still live by. Ask any good jury consultant or trial lawyer, they will tell you it's true, unfortunately.

A related tip is to keep a toiletry kit in your office, in case you have to pull an all-nighter or refresh for a late event. A toothbrush, comb, makeup, razor, and the essentials can do wonders for your sanity if you must log some serious hours.

Caren's Advice

Are you frightened now? You will not likely be pulling all-nighters often, but it will happen. In most instances, you will have the opportunity to go home, freshen up, and take a cat nap, but not always, so be prepared for the worst.

While you want to track the *type* of clothing worn by your colleagues, you should still develop your own *style*. Now may be the first time that you have thought about a style; it can also be the perfect opportunity to remake yourself. Like it or not, people make many judgments based on looks. In addition, it can be fun to develop some element of style that sets you apart from the crowd, perhaps with accessories like scarves, ties, socks, or jewelry. Maybe you collect fountain pens or cufflinks that can be part of your style. Use resources such as knowledgeable sales clerks, girlfriends, boyfriends, or others to create your personal signature.

Some things are no brainers: wear up-to-date glasses; choose a sensible haircut; keep clothes cleaned and pressed; wear several pairs of shoes; don't flaunt tattoos or out of the ordinary piercings; don't dress like you are going to a hot night club or to a funeral (unless you are a probate attorney, see above); find your razor and use it; wear modest amounts of perfume; and above all, avoid things that obviously might offend for whatever reason. Dress how you want to be perceived by you new colleagues—sharp and professional.

A close friend from law school—we'll call him John—was a brilliant lawyer, graduated magna cum laude. His sister was a television actress, yet he had the worst wardrobe; really even beyond the flannel lumberjack shirt and Wrangler jeans look. He actually came to class a few times wearing his shirts inside out. I visit him every couple of years and the amazing thing is he still wears the same casual clothes from law school! John specializes in white collar crime at a major national firm, but before starting the job, the actress sister dragged him to Brooks Brothers and forced John to buy five dark suits, ten white shirts and several conservative ties. While failure to dress for success is not a felony, it can invite a ticket from the fashion police.

To avoid a citation, like John, you will have to shop for new clothes. While this might be a hardship in light of student loans, think of your wardrobe as an investment. However, don't go overboard; being perceived as a clothes horse or a dandy may be just as damaging as being a slob. In a business casual firm, you should have a minimum of three formal outfits, suits or combos. If you are in a city with large temperature swings, you may need lighter summer attire, as well. Always keep your wardrobe updated and fresh. If you do not like to shop or have no eye for style, bring along a friend or relative who can give you honest opinions.

Caren's Advice

One last comment regarding dressing for events. Dress up because you can always dress down. In other words, if you are not sure about attire for the event, wear a tie and just take it off it the majority of men are in button-downs. For ladies, wear a suit, and remove the suit jacket if the event turns out to be business casual.

Next, what about your car? The chances are you will need one. If you live and work in Boston, Chicago, DC, New York City, or San Francisco, you may have an excuse not to own a car. Elsewhere, people will think it odd that you do not have your own wheels. The environmental merits of this can be saved for another day. The rule for cars is that you want something nice, but not too nice. A brand new Mercedes will send the wrong message just as will a beat-up Buick. You must keep the interior of your car clean, no mass of fast food wrappers and dirty gym gear. I guarantee that there will be a time when you must drive a partner or client, and the message of driving a dirty wreck is not one you want to send.

Another rule of thumb is that you don't want a car that is nicer than the partners' cars. With this in mind, it's OK to have a fussy classic Porsche that you maintain, but not a brand new six-figure turbo model. Your car can be fun and even quirky, if it has class. It's fine if the old BMW model 2002 is finicky, but driving the hand-me-down Pontiac Sunbird is a no-no (it never had class, not even when new).

Like clothes, your car should project an image that you find comfortable. There was an associate I worked with who drove a run-down entry level car for years. He was a sharp dresser, a good lawyer who made a nice salary, but he turned into a slob when driving to and from the office. No one thought of him as sensible, he was seen as a cheapskate and the car became the butt of many jokes. Why subject yourself to that?

Even if you have a car, public transportation is often the best way to travel. When you take the commuter train in particular, or the bus/subway/L to a lesser degree, always wait on the same platform, ride in the same car, sit in the same seating area, and try to catch the same train or bus every day, at least in the morning. Why? In the ordinary course, you will become commuting "buddies" with the business folks in your coach. You don't know where this will lead, but it is a free networking opportunity that you shouldn't miss. It may take you a few tries to find a spot you like, so survey the situation and move around some before you settle in. The same applies for using day lockers at the health club and similar repetitive situations.

A very good friend and former law partner has ridden in the same train, same car, same schedule, from the North Shore suburbs to downtown Chicago for the past twenty years. Over time, he became friendly with the business people who also commuted to the city. The group would know who boarded at what stops as well as each other's work and family lives. Naturally, friendships and business relationships developed over the course of time. After all, they lived in the same towns and were business guys commuting to the city. It helped that, on the way home, the train had a bar car. Come to think of it, being in Chicago, the bar car was open on the ride in, too.

One day, a business lawyer with a small corporate insurance specialty firm, said to my friend, "Joe, I've known you for years. I think you're a creative, hardworking, and dedicated lawyer. Since my firm only does corporate work for insurance companies not litigation, I am going to refer you my best client to defend a nationwide class-action suit. The case will generate so much in billings that you will *never* be able to repay me, try as you may." My friend had a very sophisticated class-action defense practice. Sure enough, the referral resulted in literally tens of millions in legal fees over the years and helped catapult Joe's career. This connection would never have happened had my friend sat in a different train car every day.

Caren's Advice

As mentioned earlier, networking will be one of the most important core skills you will need as a lawyer. But note that networking in planes, trains, and other transportation should be approached with caution. People in certain geographic areas, say Texas for instance, are known for their gregarious nature and openness to strangers. There are, however, parts of the world where this carefree approach to small talk would not be tolerated. Having worked in Texas, and then the seemingly far-off land of New York and London, I have seen this disconnect in action. Use your people skills to decide whether or not the person next to you wants to converse. Enough said.

Now it is time for work. The next chapter explores the all-important billable hour and some fundamentals of law firm economics.

CHAPTER 5

TIME KEEPS ON SLIPPING—BILLING AND RECORD KEEPING

Billable hours are the life blood of most law firms. Even contingency fee firms will have some system to track hours to manage workload and return on investment. Your time entries on the bills are also legal writing a client is guaranteed to read. You will make hundreds, if not thousands, of time entries every year that clients and billing partners will scrutinize. Yet, no one at your firm will show you how to keep time. We can learn the basics right now.

> ### Caren's Advice
>
> If your firm offers training on timekeeping and billing, sign up. If the firm has a manual on "how to keep and bill time," read it. And if the client tells you that she has a specific requirement regarding timekeeping practices, commit it to memory.

You record billable hours on a time sheet that contains sections for client numbers, narrative, and amount of time spent. First rule, if your firm has computer timekeeping software, USE IT! I kept my time longhand for the first ten years of practice, having started work when office automation was in its infancy. It is a complete and utter waste of time to write entries longhand, have your assistant type them into a timekeeping system, you proofread, make changes, assistant retypes, then you finally submit (or "release") the time to the accounting department.

If your firm has a decent automated time entry system, you can type billing entries as you go, often using nifty shortcuts and intuitive computer aids, and you're done. Keeping time on the fly also helps you get ahead on a major chore of private practice. If you are a summer associate, now is a great time to learn the automated system, since your entries are less important and voluminous than when you start full time.

A lawyer beginning her practice these days has no reason to write time sheets longhand. You may have a learning curve with the computer system, but take it from a dinosaur like me, since everything in your life is easier on a computer—time entry will be, too. You will end up capturing more time and spending less effort on this tedious administrative chore.

Next, find out from senior associates or staff the style your firm, or the particular partners or practice groups, employs for narrative time descriptions. Nothing is more irritating—and avoidable—to the billing partner than having to change an associate's time entries for stylistic reasons. Here are a few of many things to find out.

- Does the firm favor past, present, or gerund tense for narratives, e.g., "Researched compliance with Securities Act of 1940 for new VC fund" v. "Research compliance with Securities Act of 1940 for new VC fund" v. "Researching compliance with Securities

Act of 1940 for new VC fund"?

- How are individual names handled, e.g., "Meeting with Ms. Smith" v. "Meeting with J. Smith" v. "Meeting with Jane D. Smith" v. "Meeting with Smith" v. "Meeting with JDS"?

- Does your firm generally bill in tenths or quarters of hours, 0.10s (the six minute marathon) or 0.25s? It is annoying to change 0.25s and 0.75s to 0.20s, 0.30s, 0.70s, or 0.80s, and so on.

- What level of narrative detail do the billing partners prefer? Detailed entries or short ones, e.g., "Researched Securities Act of 1940 legal issues and other filing matters for new VC fund FleeceCo Venture Partners" v. "Researched '40 Act fund formation issues"?

Caren's Advice

When in doubt about what to write, think of it from the perspective of the client. As a junior associate, this is likely your only connection to the client. The client will decide based on your time entry whether or not you add value to the case. Approach timekeeping like interviewing, be flawless.

These points will apply to most private firm timekeeping systems. The narrative portion of the time entry should generally correspond in detail to the amount of time incurred, barring unusual circumstances. For instance, it may be sufficient to simply say "Legal research" if the entry is 0.50 of an hour. However, if you spent four hours on legal research, you need more details:

"Legal research on 10th Circuit case law for 12(b)(6) motions to dismiss; review treatise and local rules on same." Keep in mind that the attorney-client privilege may be lost on narrative time entries due to downstream review by the client's nonmanagement personnel. Thus, you should avoid incriminating or embarrassing narratives. Avoid, "Confer with client on how to terminate all employees over 40 years old." Instead say, "Confer with client on strategic employment issues."

Do not assume that the billing partner is going to read every narrative you write. Therefore, it is NEVER appropriate to include internal messages in your time entries. I have seen the following *real* time entry that almost went out to a client: "Legal research for summary judgment brief—*Andy, I think I spent too much time on this because I couldn't find the right law to apply, can you review?*" Whew! The client would have flipped when he saw that. Unprofessional, careless, wasteful. Send an e-mail to the partner instead.

Caren's Advice

Other time entries to avoid: (1) "awaiting assignment"; (2) "awaiting return call from client"; (3) "reviewing client bill"; (4) "proofing for grammar and spelling"; and my personal favorite (5) "locating missing file." These are all actual time entries I have had the pleasure of dealing with during my career. And I was generous: I did not list the really, really stupid ones I have witnessed. Always ask yourself, "If I were the client, would I want to pay for this?"

Associates often ask if the meter should be running all the time, like a taxicab. You should be mindful that time entries will either be billed to your client or the partner will have to discount, or "write off," your time. Clients don't like high bills, and partners don't like time write-offs since they affect realization rate, the ratio of billed verses collected fees (which impacts profitability). If the write-off is large enough, typically over $1000, the billing partner may need approval from department or office heads. Never a fun discussion for all involved. Thus, before you start a project, get a feel from the assigning lawyer of how much time you should spend.

Obviously, if you are asked to review a truck full of documents there is the implicit expectation that you will be at it for the long haul. If you realize you cannot complete a project in the estimated period of time, don't wait until you are twenty hours over and then surprise the partner. She will think you are inefficient with no concept of delivering client value. It is better to identify the problem well beforehand, inform the partner of the situation, and ask what to do. In all likelihood, the partner may have a tip that can save time. If not, you have avoided an unpleasant surprise and appear to be conscientious of client needs. You understand the mythical "business of law."

Another way to annoy billing partners and clients is billing only in hour increments, especially eight hour slugs of time. Even if accurate, the client will think you are lazy or even deceitful. Thus, not every entry should be a round number. If you worked on drafting a brief from 8:00 a.m. to noon, a 3.6 hour entry would be more appropriate and satisfying to all involved than the 4.0 slug of time, since you probably took a break for coffee or to check e-mail anyway. Surprisingly, clients do not like to see 0.10

time entries; they believe this is nickel and diming. It's better to either not charge the client for the two minute phone call, or, better yet, aggregate a few smaller entries into a 0.30 if you can. "Telephone calls with client re '40 Act, review file materials, send follow-up e-mail. 0.30"

Time records are not only crucial for billing, they create an important journal of your work. Although you may hate keeping time, and I confess time sheet completion is a tedious chore, it is critical not to fall behind. Waiting too long to record time entries will undoubtedly result in inaccuracy and missed hours. If you cannot complete your time sheets every day, never fall more than a week behind at most. Here's a tip—as you begin or complete projects during the day, especially small things like phone calls, type (or heaven-forbid, write) at least the client and matter on the time sheet. Then at the end of the day, or when you have a breather, fill in the narrative and time spent.

If you fail to track small entries like telephone calls and e-mail responses, you will lose several hours per month in billings. Another tip is to use the "Sent Items" and "Deleted Items" features on your e-mail account, and check calendar entries to refresh your recollection of what you did on a given day. After I enter my time for a day, I will check the sent and deleted items to see if I forgot any projects. This really works! Advanced tools, like the Google Desktop Search engine, are also helpful. Search by date and see if you missed anything. If you keep a work journal or diary, a practice I advise below, you can check your notes for tasks on given days.

Let's move on to more fun things. You need a record keeping and calendar system. Luckily, Microsoft Outlook and other programs allow for the easy creation and maintenance of files and deadlines. One trick is to create folders by client, and then have your assistant scan important documents for filing in your Outlook archive. This allows you to maintain personal files that are instantly accessible. You will be a whiz on conference calls if you have this system.

I also use lab notebooks to record thoughts, telephone calls, and conversations as a work journal. Some lawyers use legal pads or spiral binders. If you are dealing with scientific or technical types, they like to see their lawyers using a lab book. There is no need to be fancy, just have a system of keeping notes that works for you. Most lawyers find one chronological log, as opposed to separate journals by client, is the easiest to manage. I keep completed journal lab books from years past and occasionally have to reference them.

Warning: There is a certain amount of snake oil that surrounds calendars and record keeping. Since most junior associates never needed a complex calendar system before their firm jobs, there is a fear of the unknown. Do not fall victim to complex, expensive external systems that someone may try to sell you. Some people, especially those from sales backgrounds, fall into a "cult of the calendar." Unless you are in a very unusual practice, the calendar software on your networked computer will be more than adequate.

Your secretary will also have to keep a chronological file of all your correspondence, expense reports, and personnel materials by month and year. You will want to have duplicates of pleadings and deal documents, but make sure to destroy things in accordance with you firm's document retention policy.

A form file is an important item to maintain for your career development. While DOCS Open and similar software make document searching much easier than in the past, there is no substitute for your own files. Your form file might have major motions, final versions of SEC filings, definitive M&A (mergers and acquisitions) documents, opinion letters, major memos, and the like. After a while, you will have many folders with samples of your work over the years, which is crucial for your personal development as a lawyer.

A final word on record keeping. You need to maintain an up to date CV or resume, including a running case or deal list. This is not because you plan to leave employment at your firm. Frequently, a client or colleague will ask for your CV as part of a new business pitch or for the representation. It is also important to have an up-to-date CV in case something unexpected happens at your firm or with your life. You never know.

A major part of your CV is a case list (for litigators) and a deal list (for transactional lawyers) or both. If you keep a running record of all your cases and deals at the time they occur, you will not have to recreate years of practice should someone request a description of your experiences. List simple and clear entries. Here is a sample section from my CV:

Andrew Hartman Case List
Federal and state cases:

Sara Lee Corp. v. Nojo Bags, Ltd. et al., U.S.D.C N.D.Ill. Case No. 97C6248 (1997). Prosecution of trademark counterfeiting case involving COACH leather goods. TRO filed and obtained.

Caterpillar Inc. v. Commissioner of Pat. & Tm., U.S.D.C N.D.Ill. Case No. 97C5208 (1997). *Appeal sub nom from In re Caterpillar Inc.*, Trademark Trial and Appeal Board of the United States Patent and Trademark Office, No. 74/404,325 (1997). Appeal from refusal of trademark registration application of Caterpillar Inc. for registration of configuration design trademark. Reported at 43 U.S.P.Q.2d 1335 (T.T.A.B. 1997).

Sara Lee Corp. v. American Leather Prods, Inc. et al., U.S.D.C N.D.Ill. Case No. 97C4158 (1997). Prosecution of trademark infringement case. Preliminary injunction obtained.

Virtual Media, Inc. v. Virtual Media Tech. Pty. Ltd., U.S.D.C N.D.Ill. Case No. 97C1405 (1997). Prosecution of declaratory judgment domain name noninfringement. Total victory after bench trial.

A detailed case or deal list speaks volumes about your practice and can be very effective for marketing. It also allows you to maintain a one-page resume with an extensive addendum about your experience. Believe me, you do not want to try and remember all your deals for the past few years—keep a running list, it will look very impressive in short order.

Caren's Advice

Be prepared to give your updated deal or case list to the marketing folks so they can use it for client pitches and to update your bio. Also, keep in mind, many partners look at the associates' bios when they are staffing their cases. Keep your case list updated and accessible at all times.

Enough of this boring stuff, let's move on the social events.

CHAPTER 6

PARTY LIKE IT'S 1999—FIRM ACTIVITIES AND EVENTS

Most lawyers are very social and outgoing, which leads to many firm parties, client events, and other functions that associates are expected to attend. These functions are important networking activities for your internal marketing and can solidify relationships with peers and superiors. It is VERY important that you attend as many events as you can, especially early in your career.

Caren's Advice

Prepare yourself. Andy is about to tell you not to drink too much or engage in any hanky-panky during firm-related events. You may experience this section as a bit patronizing. But take heed—no matter how smart you are, this can happen to you. So please read the section thoughtfully and consider his recommends so you do not become "that guy (or gal)."

First there are parties. Most firms will have various activities during the summer for summer associates and a year-end holiday party. You should ask around about which parties are "must attends" and which you could skip, if need be. Again, I encourage you to try as many events as you can to take advantage of the bonding and networking opportunities. Of course, there are some very big no-nos. The first is never ever, ever, ever, EVER get drunk. This doesn't mean don't drink. As I will discuss in the Beliefs chapter later, drinking is an important social component for many lawyers. Unless you do not consume alcohol for religious or health reasons, it is normal in most firm cultures that you will have a drink or two at parties.

To avoid getting drunk, you *must* eat before the party. Here is an unfortunate, yet common, chain of events: big holiday gala with cocktails at 6:30, dinner slated for 7:30 but actually slides to 8:00. You were pretty busy earlier at the office wrapping things up and did not have time for lunch. You arrive at the party, have one drink, then another. The alcohol hits you, and by the time dinner is served, you are already lit like the Christmas tree. As the night progresses, you get hammered, leading to dancing on the tables, hitting on the mail room clerk and mucho embarrassment. The solution? Grab a wholesome snack before the party; better yet, eat a late lunch. Insert spacers between alcoholic beverages. Spacers can be water, juice, or non-caffeinated soda pop. Above all, avoid the strong stuff unless you can handle it. Have ONE martini or whiskey, then switch to wine or beer. Remember the old adage: liquor before beer, you're in the clear. Beer before liquor, never sicker.

The problem with over-drinking is drunk people say and do stupid things. If you get drunk at a party, people will remember, you will be embarrassed, and it will affect how you are perceived for a long time. It is critical to keep in mind that while parties have social aspects, they are still business events where you must be professional. Save the heavy drinking for your fraternity and sorority reunions.

There are other things to avoid at parties. Do not look for romantic relations with colleagues, clients, or guests. This can be a career-ending move. A romantic relationship begun at a firm party is almost certainly not going to end well. If you want to roll the dice, be discrete. Most state legal ethics rules forbid sexual relations with clients; this can get you in trouble with the bar as well as the firm. Relationships with guests, such as the judge's niece Lacey, are also obvious minefields.

Another way to get into trouble at parties is the holiday skit, roast, or talent show. Avoid acts that parody or mock more senior attorneys until you have established yourself as a terrific junior associate. Even a tolerant, fun-loving partner might take something the wrong way, and you do not need a tarring. However, if you have a real talent, this could be an opportunity to stand out from the crowd. Sometimes a kitschy talent can work, but you have to be careful, avoid anything that is gross or juvenile. You want your talent to project a positive image.

Talent comes in many forms. It is quite likely that your law firm will sponsor sports teams such as softball or basketball. Even if you are not particularly athletic, you should participate in some way with these teams. Larger big-city firms will often sponsor a recreational, or fun, team as well as a serious competitive one. Choose the team that suits you. Even if you are not good at softball, still attend the games as a fan. Usually there will be a group of players and guests who retire for dinner or drinks after the game. If you can't attend the activity, find out where people are meeting and try to make an appearance. Another nice aspect of sporting events is that you can often interact with nonattorney staff in a social setting. As discussed later, positive staff relations are critical to your success, and this is a good place to get to know your colleagues and their families.

Nonathletes, like most of us, can have fun and live vicariously by joining fantasy football and baseball leagues with coworkers. This phenomenon is proving a great way for people of different ages, genders, and abilities to "play" on a level field. I have seen associates have great bonding experiences over fantasy sports leagues. NCAA basketball tournament brackets and the like are other ways to have fun with sports without breaking a sweat, so long as you don't overdo it.

If you play a social sport fairly well, like golf, tennis, paddle, or squash, you should seek out players at the firm for matches. These physical events, too, can lead to lasting bonds. Even non-competitive activities can be helpful in relationship building. At Cooley, the managing partner and many important clients are long distance trail runners. Associates who can keep up the pace have developed close personal ties resulting from shared training, post-race meals, and out-of-town events.

Some firms will have sports outings such as golf, tennis, fishing, sailing, and ski trips, which become good opportunities to network and show off your skills. Don't be afraid to compete and win, but do it in a gracious fashion. Everyone likes a winner, but not a poor sport. If you happen to be a talented golfer or tennis player, you might be sought out by partners at these events. Some partners are very competitive and see young associates as a hedge against their fading abilities.

A friend and former colleague was a professional doubles tennis player before attending law school. While not extremely successful on the circuit, he played for Stanford and was worlds above even the best amateurs in the city. A senior partner got a kick out of inviting him to his tennis club as doubles teammate for tournaments. They cleaned up. Silly? Maybe. Career advantage? For sure. The same goes for golf, squash, sailing, and other sports that rich partners and clients might enjoy.

Another key social and business event is the client lunch. When you are invited to a client lunch, especially one at a fancier restaurant or downtown club, there are a few important guidelines. First, dress professionally and up a notch from usual. Men may want to wear a suit or at least a jacket and tie. Women, don the matching combo or business dress. If you are dining at a private club, ask in advance if there is a dress code. There is nothing more embarrassing than being barred at the door for men not having a jacket and tie or for women wearing slacks (yes, there are places that formal, as Caren noted).

At the lunch, and any more formal meal, know basic table manners, order something easy to eat (not finger food), and stick with water, iced tea, or soft drinks. This is a social setting, so work on your conversation skills, inquire into the client's business and show interest. Many partners do not like to face clients or prospects alone. If you can be charming and professional, these business lunches can lead to more invitations resulting in interesting projects and relationships.

Law schools do not teach you how to perform ideally in business social events. The next chapter discusses part of the law school curriculum that is paradoxically strong and also in need of some improvement.

CHAPTER 7

(GIVE ME BACK MY) NAME—WHAT YOU WERE NOT TAUGHT IN LEGAL WRITING

Law school legal writing programs are typically very strong in traditional research skills, formal memo writing, and appellate advocacy. However, they often do not prepare you for some important aspects of everyday practice. For instance, you probably were not taught how to write the most common and important legal document—the business letter/e-mail. No doubt you practiced drafting memos and briefs, but the letter, something you will send nearly every day, was neglected. Why is this? The pedagogy of legal writing is to teach at a high skill level in the limited time available, then the students can ratchet down as needed. There is also the distrust in the academy of overemphasizing "trade" skills verses theory.

With the advent of e-mail, formal business letters are not as central to a legal practice as once upon a time, but these guidelines apply to e-mails and all written communications. There is a tendency for e-mail to become informal, which may be fine in many cases. When you are using e-mail as a substitute for a business letter, however, be formal.

A business letter must contain all important information in a short, clear opening paragraph. A client does not want wade through pages of analysis to figure out your message. In most cases, you will need to provide support for initial points, but if you bury vital information, your client will lose interest. Most clients are not trained in legal matters, are too busy, or just plain don't give a hoot about legal details. Clients want your expertise and clear guidance; some will actually suspect that a longer letter just means a bigger bill.

The visual appearance—how the letter looks on the page— is almost as important as the substance. Your letters should use short paragraphs with a lot of "air" spaces. Dense documents are difficult and daunting to read. To aid the audience, break thoughts up with bullets, diagrams, and the like whenever appropriate. Print a draft of the letter and see how it looks. Here are a few samples of concise writing.

- You are writing to notify the client about a court decision, here is an opening paragraph:

Dear Client:

Good news! We just heard from the court that your CEO will not have her deposition taken the day after Thanksgiving and you will not have to produce the box car full of confidential documents that the plaintiff demanded. I have summarized the salient points below.

- An opinion letter regarding a contract:

Dear Client:

You asked us to review the provisions of the November 4, 2005, software license agreement between your company and FleeceCo regarding whether you need to support the licensed software after the agreement expired. Based on careful analysis, it is our opinion that you do not need to support the software because FleeceCo failed to renew the services agreement. Details follow.

- Dealings with opposing counsel:

Dear Opposing Counsel:

You have noticed the deposition of Jane Smith for the day after Thanksgiving. Ms. Smith is unavailable that day. She is available any business day during the first week of December. You also asked us to provide a box car full of documents containing our client's confidential trade secrets. We cannot comply with this unreasonable request for the reasons set forth below.

- Finally, to the government:

Dear Securities and Exchange Commission:

Thank you for the comments to FleeceCo Corporation's S-1 filing. We respectfully disagree that the failure to discover the Lost City of Atlantis is a material risk requiring disclosure to potential investors. As such,

we do not believe that an amendment is warranted for
the reasons set forth below.

As you can see, you have given your client, opposing counsel,
and the government crisp and concise information in the first
paragraph of the letter. Even if the reader stops there, she will
have enough information to act. In most situations you will need
to give sufficient details to support your initial statements, but
you should tell it like it is up front. This applies to bad news that
has to be delivered by letter:

Dear Incarcerated Pro Bono Client:

I am sorry to report that the United States judge has
dismissed your case where you claim the prison's
failure to provide linen table service constitutes cruel
and unusual punishment. While I am very sympathetic
to your issues and wish it could have come out another
way, the judge simply did not agree. Below are the
details.

Back to e-mail for a minute; e-mail can be a minefield. Since
e-mail is so easily archived, so hard to delete permanently, and
simple to forward, you must NEVER say anything in e-mail that
you would not want printed on the front page of the *Wall Street
Journal*. One of my high-tech clients lost a preliminary injunction motion simply because the CEO sent one *very* improvident
e-mail. It was discovered, of course, and became Exhibit A in the
opponent's evidence.

Most of you know e-mail etiquette by now, and this is not the
place for a detailed refresher. However, there are some items that

68   NATIONAL INSTITUTE FOR TRIAL ADVOCACY

are particular to law firms. First, make sure to use the "Confidential" settings on confidential e-mail. Right? In some situations, this can prevent altering and forwarding of the e-mail. If you have something that is truly confidential, do not use e-mail at all. Use a conventional letter or pick up the telephone.

Be extremely careful when using the "Reply to All" button, as Caren noted. This is probably the genesis of most e-mail gaffs. Some firms have installed a prompt that asks, "Are you sure you want to reply to all?" You should act as if that prompt exists and hesitate before sending. Instead of using buttons to reply or reply to all, I use the Outlook shortcuts control-R (reply) or control-shift-R (reply to all), in order to reduce slips of the finger.

Another question that arises is how to handle jokes and questionable media that you may receive from friends or colleagues via e-mail or message. Remember, your computer and e-mail account (and firm-issued cell phone or PDA) belong to the firm, and you have no expectation of privacy therein. Unless the joke is something you wouldn't be embarrassed sharing with your mother, do not forward. You may need to read it to see what is actually there (and this may give you some satisfaction), but if it is offensive in any way, do not forward using firm resources.

One way around this situation is to maintain a free e-mail account such as Hotmail, G-mail or Yahoo!mail, unless your firm has a policy that prohibits such software on your office computer. Even with these accounts, you must assume that all communications using the firm's network can and will be reviewed by firm administration at some point. Communications on your personal e-mail account can help segregate work from fun, but please note that even e-mail use on a personal account can be monitored, recorded, and summarized since the data travels through the firm's firewall. If there is something that you absolutely would not want scrutinized, do not use your office computer network.

Many firms will have an e-mail clown or two. Most of the clown's communications will be benign and maybe even amusing. When you receive mailings from the e-mail clown, you can read them, but forwarding an off-color joke puts you in the soup just as the person who originally sent it. It is best that you not become a clown until you have established a stellar reputation for high quality work, if then.

While e-mail and letters are a major part of your practice, briefs, memos, and deal documents will cover most of your significant legal drafting duties. In that regard, our next topic is forms and reinventing the wheel. Most firms will have a document management system that allows you to pull precedential documents that can be the basis of your current drafting projects. This is a fine thing to do. Some firms will have a set form file that associates are expected to utilize.

When using forms, it is crucial that you *conform* the document to the particular matter. There is nothing more embarrassing than turning in projects that contain vestiges from prior deals or cases. Make use of the "find" and "replace" features on your word processing software and be sure to proof read carefully. If you are not a careful reader, enlist someone who is. Do not make the mistake of leaving vestiges or nonconforming language in your legal documents—it shows sloppiness and is easily cured.

Caren's Advice

Not to belabor this point, but please make sure you have changed the name of the client on the form and that the client name is spelled correctly.

Conforming also includes a document's internal reference to particular numbered paragraphs, exhibits, tables, and the like. When referencing a numbered paragraph, it is good practice to leave the reference blank until you are ready to produce a final draft to the partner. They you fill in the blanks and everything fits together nicely. It is maddening and shows carelessness if your internal references do not align.

If you are not a strong writer, consider taking a course at a local college, legal trainer, or the bar association. While the firm may sponsor such a course, you may not want to wait for it to be scheduled. If you are really struggling with writing, make an investment in yourself. To succeed as a lawyer in private practice, you will have to be at least a decent writer. Associates who have the reputation of excellence in writing are often sought out for important projects. If you are a poor writer, you will not only be dinged on reviews, you will never be tapped for important written projects.

Caren's Advice

Your ability to write well will make or break your career. If you have EVER received any negative feedback on your writing, ask the partner or someone from the

> professional development department for help. Most firms employ external writing coaches who will work one-on-one with you over time to enhance your skills.

Whatever your writing skills, there are some things that senior attorneys find very aggravating. You must know and obey basic grammatical rules. These are subject-verb agreement, comma and semicolon usage, plurals, proper verb tense conjugation, possessives, homonym use (e.g., its v. it's; their, they're, and their; your v. you're; principle v. principal; affect v. effect) and other basic elements. These are mistakes you can easily avoid by purchasing a copy of Strunk and White's *The Elements of Style* and using it. Another good resource is the ALI/ABA publication *Plain and Accurate Style in Court Papers*, by Irwin Alterman.

In addition, make sure that you also have a good dictionary and thesaurus on your desk and online. A particularly good synonym finder is McMillan Publishing's *Legal Thesaurus* by William C. Burton. Many other good resources for writing can be found in your library or bookstore or online. There are great resources on the Web, but have a least one good dictionary on your shelf.

The most important admonition is PROOFREAD, PROOFREAD, PROOFREAD! Simply put, only turn in documents to senior lawyers that are in final form, ready for filing, unless told otherwise explicitly. Your papers will be edited by senior lawyers and clients of course, but don't give the appearance of being lazy or sloppy by relying on others to catch your errors. Above all else, use spell check, but never rely on it exclusively—you must proofread after spell checking, and if you are not a careful proofreader, get help. A friendly colleague can catch common mistakes. Find a proofreading buddy at the firm and exchange drafts for review.

Caren's Advice

In addition to proofreading, make it "pretty." Include all of the necessary formatting so that it can go directly to the client, court, or other recipient without any additional work.

A few more considerations about legal writing warrant attention. As I discussed earlier, keep samples of your work in a personal form file. You can then tap these forms for future assignments, reference material, or if you need to provide examples of your writing. Writing well is something you can only learn by doing; there is no substitute for on-the-job training. If you do not hone your writing skills early in your legal career, you will become stunted. While oral advocacy is usually more fun than brief writing, make sure to keep up a regular flow of written work.

It is also important to develop a flexible writing style depending on the audience. Most of the time you will want to avoid overly complex sentence structures, uncommon word choices, extraneous adjectives and adverbs, and especially *Latin*. You may need to use a Latin term when it is a legal doctrine, like *res ipsa loquitur* or *nunc pro tunc*. It is also appropriate to use very common Latin terms like *inter alia*, *supra*, and *infra*. However, avoid showing how smart you are by throwing around arcane Latin terms to describe legal theories or situations.

Black's Law Dictionary is chock-full of annoying Latin expressions that some of your law school professors loved. Will your average state court judge know what *a summo remedio ad inferiorem actionem non habetur regressus neque auxilium* means? How about a more common one, *inclusio unius est exclusio alterius*? You are close enough to law school to remember that one from contracts class, but why test the judge and force her to pull out Black's? Just say "by including one you necessarily exclude the other." The hocus-pocus overuse of Latin is a major error that many junior lawyers make. *Finis.*

In contrast, the opposite of using too much Latin is being too folksy. Folksiness is like salt—a little can add flavor, too much ruins the meal. If you are not a folksy person, don't force it, and if your practice is very formal, informality will not work. You can be a little folksy if every other part of your writing is perfect. If not, you're viewed as a hayseed, not a creative writer. You should also avoid incredibly overused colloquialisms like, "that dog won't hunt," or "until the cows come home."

To pull off folksy metaphors you will need to match illustrative phrases to your particular situation. It may be appropriate to say that "the Company's CEO spends money like a sailor on leave" in a shareholder derivative suit, but not in a private placement offering.

Another persuasive writing strategy is to identify items of pop culture when the reader was in high school or college and use them sparingly in examples and analogies as appropriate. For instance, the judge assigned to your case attended Berkeley in the 1960s. You may be able to weave in references to music and events of the era that had an indelible impact during her critical formative years.

You can also learn something about the reader's background or interests, like golf or theatre, and use that information in your materials. One of Cooley's best litigation associates includes sports metaphors that correspond with the season when he knows the judge is a fan. The plaintiff's third motion on the same issue was his "third strike" in the spring, but would have been a "Hail Mary pass" in the fall. There is a danger of pandering, so, again, be sparing in applying this type of flare.

The discussion on flare and folksiness are examples to show legal writing need not be boring. In fact, some of the best writers meld impeccable basic skills with appropriate flourishes. Your written product will never be effective if it is dull or lacks substance. Your target should be an error-free document with clear and accurate style that emphasizes the fundamentals with some added interest.

CHAPTER 8

LOSING MY RELIGION—BELIEFS AND BACKGROUND

Enough serious stuff. Let's turn to benign subjects like religion, race, gender, and beliefs. Hopefully none of the items discussed below will ever become an issue for you, not because you fit in the mainstream of your law firm, but because you will distinguish yourself on quality of work, not your background. This section might seem farfetched with the nation's general increase in tolerance and firms' desire for diversity. However, some people can harbor unfortunate biases that could affect your career. Historically, many large law firms were founded by individuals of certain ethnic backgrounds, and some firms have kept their character to this day.

No matter what the firm's ethnic history and mix, nearly every large law firm will have a policy that embraces all religions, races, and beliefs, and forbids discrimination. If you find yourself in a situation where there is an *institutional* bias against you due to a trait protected by law, get out! Planning your exit might take some time, and you may need to seek the advice of qualified counsel. The exit period could be uncomfortable, but just get out as fast as you can! Laudable as it might be, you will NOT be able to change the institution from the inside as a junior lawyer. Bias by *individuals* is another story.

Hopefully, your research and recon on the background of firm attorneys will identify both senior lawyers who you should embrace and those whom you should avoid (for whatever reason). Although a civil rights activist might say otherwise, usually the best advice is to avoid situations before problems occur, rather than trying to face them head on. Traversing a problem, if possible, is preferred over direct conflict. For example,

- if there is a lawyer who has the reputation of working very late into the night and you have a new baby at home, you may find it best to avoid working with this attorney until your child is older and more independent, or until you have proven yourself to be a great associate and can arrange a more flexible schedule, or until you have adequate child care.

- if you do not work on certain days for religious reasons and there is a lawyer who requires that her associates be available say Sunday to meet with her Japanese client for regular Monday morning (Japan time) teleconferences, perhaps avoid her until you have established yourself and can work around the situation.

Both of these examples show a degree of insensitivity, rather than outright discrimination. Until you have gained the confidence of your colleagues, these situations will place you in an uncomfortable position that could easily be avoided. Should the firm do better in these situations? Of course. Is it your job as a junior associate fresh out of law school to force the issue? Probably not. As you develop, gain skills and respect, you can be a voice for positive change.

If you believe there is a real harassment problem with a more senior attorney, my advice is first a reality check. Speak with an honest, reasonable confidant outside the firm and determine if you are seeing things clearly. If your belief is affirmed, you have several choices, none of which are great.

In the back of your mind you should always ask, "Can I get through this?" There might be reasons you say no. You might be in a fragile emotional or financial state, for instance. The next question is what are your reasonable goals? Do you want to stay at the firm and try to make it work? Do you want the wrongdoer disciplined? Do you want compensation for harm? Do you want to just be done with the firm and move on?

Your actions should be in accordance with your goals, not your emotions of the moment. If you think there can be a positive change and you want to work things out, you should seek advice from a more senior friend or mentor at the firm. It's likely that the firm will have some sort of diversity or nonharassment committee. If you inform a committee member, or even any partner/manager, of the situation, an investigation and formal firm process will likely be set in motion.

There is no such thing as an "informal" complaint. Ask yourself, does an investigation align with my goals? I can't give you the answer to this very difficult problem other than to advise you to be aware of your goals and your particular situation before you take any action (or *decide* upon nonaction). An allegation of harassment is nearly impossible to unmake. That could be the correct course for you, but determine whether you are certain about your concerns and think as many moves ahead as possible.

How about issues considered by most as less serious than race, gender, religion, sexual orientation, national origin, etc., that fall into the category of personal preferences not protected by law? Perhaps you are vegetarian (for nonreligious reasons) in a carnivorous city like Chicago, Kansas City, or Dallas. You don't drink alcohol for nonreligious or nonhealth related reasons. You are a Cal grad at a firm pervaded with Stanford alumni. All of these can be nonissues and could actually be positives if handled well. Don't feel you have to compromise on your preferences to fit in.

The rule of thumb is don't be annoying about your feelings, whatever they are. If you are a vegetarian, don't announce it stridently, chastise your peers for eating cute, lovable- creatures, or make a big fuss about where the gang has lunch. When you go out, simply order something meatless. Eventually, someone will ask and people will figure it out. By then they will know you, and your food preferences won't be a big deal for anyone. This strategy can be applied to more serious food consumption management, such as Kosher, Halal, Hindu, food allergies, or medically related dietary restrictions, like diabetes. Do what you need and want to do, but be relaxed about it.

One exception to this laid back attitude is if you are invited to a partner's or client's home for dinner. If you surprise your host or hostess by not eating an elaborately prepared beef Wellington because you are vegan, or the scallops Coquille St. Jacque because you keep Kosher or Halal, your host will feel uncomfortable and embarrassed.

In this day and age, with so many people on one diet or another, your host will probably ask if there is anything you do not eat ahead of time. Take the opportunity to explain the situation pleasantly, but don't make a fuss. Not only will the host enjoy making an alternative meal, he will be proud of the effort and self-laud the thoughtfulness. If the host does not give you the courtesy of a diet inquiry, don't wait for the inevitable embarrassing situation to occur; pleasantly mention your restrictions in advance.

What if you don't drink alcohol? As mentioned earlier, alcohol looms very large at most firm social events. By not partying with the gang at Friday happy hour or skipping firm events, you will miss out on important networking and bonding opportunities; then if you say no often enough, you will not be asked again. If you don't drink alcohol for whatever reason, just be laid back about it and still attend social functions. One of my former partners who does not drink alcohol attends almost every firm party and drinks soda with lime. It looks like a cocktail, he never makes a big deal out of it, and that's that.

You shouldn't hide the fact that you don't drink (or worse, sacrifice beliefs just to fit in), but like food observances, eschewing drinking alcohol can be a nonissue if handled well. A strategy to avoid some misguided, yet friendly, colleague pushing a cocktail on you and possibly creating an uncomfortable situation is to always have a full soft drink in your hand. That way when asked, you can simply say, "I'm fine, thanks." Like the vegetarian and Kosher/Halal examples, eventually people will get to know you and this will not be a source of any concern. Soon everyone will ask the abstainers for drink tickets when there is a cash bar. And you will be the toast of the event!

While food and drink might seem basic or marginal to your success at the firm, little things do affect development. With some planning and forethought you should be able to fit in with your colleagues without sacrificing your values or becoming a Stepford associate.

Unfortunately, firm life is not just partying. Between social events, you will have to do a large amount of work to succeed and develop skills. The next chapter discusses some ways to keep sane while keeping plenty busy.

CHAPTER 9

THERE IS NO TIME—MANAGING YOUR LIFE

Billable hours are the bread and butter of most private law firms. These hours represent the firm's production. Billables cover most overhead and, hopefully, result in profits. Remember, profits do not just benefit partners. A portion of profits is typically channeled into the associate bonus pool. The biggest chunk of overhead is payroll, and the biggest portion of payroll is associate compensation. Thus, hours are so critically important in almost all firms and for your contribution thereto that you must know expectations.

Most big firms expect associates to bill approximately 165 to 200 client chargeable and collectable hours per month or between 1950 and 2400 hours per year. There are variations based on geography, culture, and practice. While your firm might have a stated minimum, or goal, you need to determine what's *really* expected. At some firms, the stated policy is actually the expected policy. In others, you will be dinged if you "only" reach the goal; in other words, it is the bare minimum. You need to know what is really expected, then keep in line with, or exceed, your peers.

If possible, you want to be *at least* in the middle of the pack with your peers in terms of billing, or higher if you want to stand out. The middle may be hard to ascertain since you won't have access to the hours numbers of your cohort at most firms. As a general rule, if you are consistently in the 175 per month range you should be fine at typical firms, except for the real sweat shops.

Even if the firm does not publish peer hours, you will be able to gather general information from partners in your practice group. As you work, continue to find out exactly what is expected of you by gathering data and then determining where you fit in with your cohorts. A stated goal of 170 hours per month may not cut if everyone else is at 200, no matter what the firm reported to NALP.

There was a great letter to *The Rodent* newsletter back in the early 1990s from a frazzled associate. *The Rodent* had its beginnings as an underground newsletter that was photocopied and physically circulated around law firms. It ultimately became more mainstream. It was the *Above the Law* of its day. I will paraphrase here:

> Every day the befuddled associate would start and stop a stopwatch, recording time according to the work he conducted for clients. The associate was concerned because at the end of a full twelve hour day, he could only account for half the time in billable hours. Yet, everyone else around him worked the same amount of time, or less, but billed ten hours or more. The associate asked what he was doing wrong.

The Rodent offered the advice that the associate should do what experienced lawyers do: start the stopwatch when he wakes up, stop it when he goes to bed, calculate the total hours, and divide by the clients' ability to pay.

Humorous, yes. Accurate, not really. But there is a grain of truth to everything. This letter got a friend and ex-law partner in trouble when he was a junior associate at a major Silicon Valley firm. My friend, enjoying a good reputation, but known as a joker, showed *The Rodent* letter to a partner who laughed and said the firm should circulate it to the summer associates. Thinking that all associates might appreciate the humor, he sent the letter via a written memo to the associates, lauding the efficiency of *The Rodent's* billing philosophy. He then left on vacation.

The joker's friends tried to stop distribution of the memo. When he checked in for voice messages, there was an ominous recording from the managing partner suggesting that someone might be playing a joke on him by circulating the memo under his name. This was pre-e-mail, so every associate at the firm had actually received a paper memo with the article.

My friend fessed up to the joke and enlisted the aid of the partner who suggested he send the memo around, but always suspected he might be tarnished by the incident. Interestingly, the *Wall Street Journal* picked up on the story and wrote a report with the last sentence stating that eight months later the associate left his firm for reasons "unrelated" to the memo. He now laughs and says, "Unrelated, but symptomatic."

Moving on to real time management, as noted above, using a computerized time entry system can assist you greatly in capturing hours so you don't need *The Rodent's* method. As a junior associate, it is important to record all, or nearly all, of your time even if you feel the day was not spent as efficiently as it could have been. Until you know the firm's billing practices and determine how long projects should take, it does no good to shortchange yourself out of hours.

An associate should communicate with the assigning attorneys when he senses that he is spending more hours on a project than necessary. Although this is not easy to gauge, time budgeting will come with experience. Perhaps the only exception to recording all or nearly all time accrued is when you have truly blown an assignment—if you did not understand what law to apply, forgot a key fact, or floundered with an obsolete template. This will hopefully never happen, but if it does, simply chalk the effort up to experience, don't include the time, and move on. Recording the time, then informing the partner of the mistake, may not serve you in the long run.

Billing is obviously important and so is managing your workload. Most associates receive projects from many different people who are not aware of the associate's caseload. In any event, keep a full plate of work and err on the side of taking on a little too much. It is dangerous to turn down assignments unless you are billing 200 per month for the managing partner's clients; then you are in position to fend off additional work. If you are in the middle or lower part of the pack for hours, the expectation is that you always can and should do more.

Almost never say no to work. Manage due dates and juggle the best you can. The view of most partners is that associates are paid a lot and need to produce a lot of hours to make firm economics work. Also, most partners were very hard workers as junior associates and expect the same from you. You will often hear partners say that associates these days don't have the same work ethic as years ago. Certainly partners for decades have been saying that about their generation of associates. Rather than debate this, try your best not to be the target of such ridicule.

Once you accept a project, finish it!

Caren's Advice

And on time! If you don't think you can make the deadline, tell the partner before the deadline occurs, not when it occurs. Some partners offer you the same deadline they have, thus there is not much room for delay between when you give it to them and when they give it to the client or the court.

This obvious rule is often not followed. Nothing is worse for a manager than having a project boomerang or receiving something incomplete or done poorly. Although at times it may be better to say no to work than to do a poor job, it is best to manage everything to successful completion even if it requires long hours.

Often dates can be shuffled around to even out work flow. You can usually change times for depositions, meetings, and the like, if need be. In a real crunch, you can even change most court dates and extend most deadlines. Make sure you clear things with senior attorneys first, but don't be afraid to manage your practice if your colleagues and clients are amenable. In fact, practice and time management are two important associate review factors in most firms. The ability to change dates shows that you can manage a complex practice effectively.

In addition to billable hours, there will be the expectation that you contribute some time to internal firm activities. These can include recruiting, pro bono matters, and marketing. This work may actually be more interesting than your client chargeable time. Always bear in mind, however, that big firm economics are built around billable hours. Thus, you will need a solid foundation of client chargeable hours in addition to any nonbillable activities.

Even if your firm gives full or partial billing credit for certain worthy activities, like pro bono, you still need solid chargeable hours to maintain a comfortable position among your peers. While the firm recognizes that nonbillable hours can ebb and flow depending on pro bono litigation activity or during the fall on campus interview season, you do not want to have a year after year imbalance between your client chargeable billings and nonbillable hours. You will get a reputation that is hard to shake.

Caren's Advice

Time spent on training also typically falls into the nonbillable category for most firms. Think of this time as an investment in your career. The more experience and training you have, the more prepared you will be to grow and advance in your practice. Pro golfers do not get any credit for the time they spend practicing, they only get credit for wins. The same is true for lawyers; your "credit" is advancement in the profession, which often results in a higher salary and, hopefully, partnership opportunities.

With all these hours demands, how do you manage your personal life? As you seek a balance between work and outside activities, you must understand that the private practice of law at a big firm calls for significant personal sacrifice. This is particularly true in the first few years when you have less control over time and are still proving yourself. The reward is high pay, ample support, professionalism, independence, mobility, and career development. Unfortunately, in most practices work comes in fits and starts rather than at a constant flow. If you have a vacation planned and your main client is hit with a TRO (temporary restraining order) or enters into an unexpected M&A transaction, your schedule will have to change. You need to be flexible.

At times you may find yourself simply overwhelmed with work that you just cannot handle. If this happens, communicate the situation to your senior colleagues and suggest a solution. You could request that another associate or paralegal work with you. Consider stretching deadlines and tapping additional resources; sometimes a good secretary and document processing department can relieve a lot of your pressure. When you can't return a call in a timely manner (within an hour or so) at least have your secretary notify the caller that you are tied up. The same applies to e-mails; send a reply to the client or senior lawyer simply saying that you received the message and will review as soon as possible. The key here is to recognize a problem, communicate effectively, and have a solution that makes sense.

Caren's Advice

No matter the circumstances, always respond with a follow-up phone call or e-mail regardless of how much time has passed. In my former AmLaw 100 firm, several partners were tasked with monitoring the development of the associates in their group. Throughout the year, the partners would e-mail each associate to request a meeting to discuss her developmental progress and needs. Would you believe that many associates never responded? If you miss an e-mail, respond with your sincere apology ASAP; most people will understand.

You will have the flexibility to look better, or worse, when it comes to hours. When I was a junior associate at a patent boutique firm, one of the big shot partners was an early riser. He would always be in by 7:00 a.m. and leave at about 5:00. I would try to arrive at 8:00 or earlier to be available. One of the other associates, a very hard worker, just couldn't get out of the house early and would roll in after 9:00 and sometimes closer to 10:00. As time went by, this grated more and more on the senior partner. It didn't matter that the associate routinely worked past midnight. It didn't matter that he was a good lawyer. What mattered was that his office was dark and it was on the path between the entrance and the senior partner's office.

I could swear that the senior partner kept a log, clocking when the associate arrived each morning, rather than reviewing the associate's actual time reports. This was a factor in my colleague's eventual departure from the firm. What could he have done? I honestly believe he was clueless about the negative impact caused by his late arrival. If he had been more aware, he could have struggled to arrive early or at least by nine.

Caren's Advice

And if you arrive early (or stay late) similar to the partner's schedule, you may be privy to informative "big picture" discussions about the case that do not take place regularly in the heat of the day.

What if you simply cannot arrive early? Not because you are lazy, but because you have family responsibilities. One option is to discuss the situation with the senior partner. However, this may define you as an excuse maker. Instead, think outside the box. Send voice mails and e-mails with late night time indicators to show the partner that you work quite late. Volunteer to help on matters where you need to deal with counsel in the Far East or Australia, or even in California if your firm is on the East Coast, thereby having a valid reason to keep late hours. Think about trading offices with an early riser who might like the exposure to Mr. or Ms. Big. These might seem silly or farfetched, but if confronted with a situation try to develop a creative solution.

What you should *not* do is have your secretary or a colleague log onto your computer, thus "punching you in" early. This smacks of fraud and if discovered could result in discipline. Similarly, think twice about even having someone turn on your lights, although this is more benign and even expected if you leave items in an outbox for early morning processing. If you ask your secretary to turn on your lights, this will eventually work its way through the grapevine, so have some reasonable justification for it or simply avoid the issue.

On the flip side, some associates have turned the staging of their offices to indicate late night activities into an art form. Forget just leaving a light on after you leave. I have seen associates actually leave sweaters and jackets on their chairs, shoes under their desks and timer radios playing to indicate late night occupancy. One sly associate would leave an old handbag, obviously one not containing any valuables, on her desk to stage her presence after leaving the office hours earlier. Using office technology you can also leave delayed voice mails and e-mails for partners. Of course, I would never condone such behavior.

As hard as it may be, you do have to make time for yourself, this is another investment in the future. If you don't make "me" time, you will either burn out dramatically or have a long miserable career. You can fit in personal time in many ways. Even when you are really busy, a simple walk to the park or a quick lunch with a friend can recharge the batteries.

Athletics and fitness are very important. This can take the form of organized sports or be as simple as increasing the amount of steps you walk each day. Many lawyers enjoy exercising at lunch and then grabbing a sandwich to eat on the way back to the office. No time for the gym? A friend who is the managing partner of a large firm had a goal of walking five miles in the ordinary course of a day since he had no time to exercise. There are about 2000 steps per mile. He bought a cheap pedometer. My friend would park the car in the end of the lot, use stairs not the elevator, walk instead of cab to meetings when he could, go the long way to a colleague's office, and do a dozen other things. This might seem trivial, but it can keep you sane and healthy, and he had a goal.

Another friend would take what he called an "executive work-out," a sauna and shower, when he didn't have time for a full exercise routine, in order to recharge. It took only about twenty minutes, and left him feeling great. The name of the game is to do something to relieve stress, refresh yourself, and keep sane. The practice of law is a marathon in six-minute segments, not a sprint. Don't burn out.

CHAPTER 10

PUT ME IN COACH, I'M READY TO PLAY—TEAMWORK, MANAGING UP AND DOWN

Good law firms strive to be like winning sport teams. There are tryouts and challenges, shake outs and surprise endings; over time, those who are disinterested in a team approach or are unable to cope generally don't stick around. A team is not necessarily a democracy, though, or a place for group hugs. Teams have leaders and subordinates, stars and grinders. The key is that everyone on the team has an important role to play.

The analogy to team sports or other coordinated group efforts such as theatre, choir, orchestra, or a band is actually very apt. I have known lawyers *at all levels* who had never participated in team efforts during school years who failed at big law firms. Being a part of a team teaches you the need for support, trust, delegation, and, above all, humility. Anyone who has tried out for a competitive sports team, theatre production, or choir knows failure and learns from it. Most of us were not an all-American quarterback, perennial lead in the high school play, first violin, or drum major in the marching band.

Paradoxically, it is *humility* and need for support that gives you the *confidence* to succeed in private practice. If you are too cocky and think you can go it alone, you will miss out on valuable intelligence gathering, mentoring, and support from friends and colleagues. If you never faced any hardship in your life, be it actual struggles or competitive challenges, you will not know when you are in trouble or when you need help.

How does this team metaphor play out with your colleagues? No matter how hard we try to keep an open mind, nearly all of us have experienced an almost instant dislike for someone at some point in our lives. Sometimes the dislike is due to jealousy or unfamiliarity, but I would offer that most cases result from the other person's failure to be part of the team, to fit in at least to some extent. You do not want to be the object of scorn for being such a person.

Who is on your team and what is your role? As a new lawyer, you will be in a difficult situation right from the beginning; you will have more authority, more independence, and earn higher wages than most (or all) nonlawyers at the firm, such as secretaries, paralegals, and clerks, who have been there longer than you. This can build resentment, and subordinates can subtly undermine your practice. You need to treat everyone on the team—staff, peers, and superiors—with respect. By doing this, you will avoid most unpleasant situations and gain valuable allies as the years go by. Most people find it easy to manage up (please the boss) but difficult to manage down (incentivize, support, comfort, and motivate subordinates). Both are equally important.

It is not difficult to understand your role relative to partners and other senior attorneys. Your goal is to become a valued junior member of the team. As I described before, your job early on is to produce superlative work and show your superiors potential for becoming an outstanding lawyer. As always, you need to know your audience. Most senior lawyers at your firm will not demand or want sycophantic obsequiousness, but they will expect some amount of deference. The amount depends on the person, and you need to know his boundaries. In my experience, associates who best integrate with partners and senior lawyers are those who become friends or friendly through shared interests and activities. Someone once characterized this as "dating" the senior attorneys. The dating does not result in improper relationships, but it is another apt observation. You want the senior lawyers to like working with you for who you are and for what you have to offer. This is also akin to the time-honored Dale Carnegie theory of sales—customers become friends and friends become customers.

How do you accomplish this? Begin by using your energy and enthusiasm to improve the social aspects of your job with a side benefit of networking. The key is to pursue *your* interests, and involve others. If you are a motorcycle rider, find other bikers and go for weekend rides. By including clients this becomes a marketing opportunity. The same goes for running, biking, and other so-called individual sports. Games and music work well, too. See who wants to attend a concert or play pool after work, organize a bridge, hearts, poker or euchre group. I have friends and clients who regularly visit BBQ joints for lunch. Be inclusive and invite your peers as well as superiors. Networking happens when you least expect it. When you involve yourself in the lives of your colleagues, you will find work more enjoyable and you will integrate more easily.

Above all, dismiss the attitude that you shouldn't socialize with coworkers, that you have plenty of friends from school and growing up, and that you want to separate work from free time. This is the kiss of death. You will be perceived as a prima donna and will not fit in with the firm. You do not need to be best pals with everyone at the office, but don't go the opposite route either.

In addition to forming bonds with clients, peers, and superiors, do not overlook the staff and subordinates as assets and allies. Obviously, your secretary (or assistant) and paralegals can have a direct impact on your career—positive and negative. Without a doubt, many secretaries and paralegals have substantial legal skills, and they have networked successfully within the firm. These nonattorneys can be very influential. They often assist partners in deciding how to staff cases; their feedback could even be sought on associate reviews.

In addition, other staff in the firm can be an immense asset from time to time. Docket clerks, mail room personnel, the copy department, document processing, receptionists, and librarians can make your job easier, or they can undermine you in subtle and not so subtle ways. If you are a jerk to the copy department, your job will somehow find itself at the bottom of the pile. Receptionists can cover for you when you're at the gym, or they can say, "Gee Ms. Partner, that associate always seems to disappear for hours during the middle of the day. Wonder where he goes." This happens.

In addition to firm staff, you will deal with outside service providers of all types. These people come in and out of your life and can be very helpful. In some circumstances you can actually learn a lot from even those whom junior lawyers would not believe could be helpful. When I first started at Cooley one of our Silicon Valley dot-com clients was sued by a large automaker in

Detroit. The head of our litigation department knew I was born in Detroit and asked me to pitch in.

It was a big case and I was on the spot to do well, to prove myself, even as a partner. Upon reading the complaint, it was apparent that there was no personal jurisdiction over the start-up in Eastern Michigan. I moved to dismiss the case and flew to Detroit for the hearing. The automaker tried to home court us with every trick in the book, including the sudden appearance on the court papers of a junior associate who was a former law clerk of the judge.

The judge is an African-American woman who was a former Detroit city councilwoman. As I rode the taxi from the airport to downtown Detroit, we passed through Dearborn and the Ford headquarters, the Henry Ford Memorial Hospital, and the UAW headquarters. My confidence started to slip. The driver was an older African-American gentleman in his 60s, the judge's vintage. He was chatty and asked what brought me to Detroit dressed in a fancy grey chalk-striped suit. I told him a little about the case and asked his opinion about how the judge would feel about the auto company. I had owned its cars and believed the manufacturer had a pretty solid reputation.

The driver felt differently and began a half hour dissertation about how some black Detroiters felt its founder was a racist who put black factory workers in the worst jobs, shoveling coal and in the steel mills, never on the assembly line. During his time, most of the company's management was white. He was confident that the judge, his contemporary, would feel the same way. This buoyed my confidence. I argued the case and the next day the judge dismissed the complaint for lack of personal jurisdiction.

Did the driver help us win the motion? Perhaps. At the very least he was a friend in enemy territory who raised my spirits.

Another way staff can help you when you go to the gym, extend your lunch, or take personal time during the day: let your secretary know when you will be back and request him to say you are out on an appointment, or are unavailable, and can be reached by mobile phone. A senior partner at my old firm always had his secretary say he was at the *court* whenever he went to play squash (squash *court*—get it?). It was an inside joke for those who knew him, seemed impressive to those who didn't, and it wasn't even a lie!

As a side bar, don't be afraid to do "secretarial" work when you need to. It is critical to know how to e-file, operate the copy machine, scanner, fax machine, postage meter, and other support equipment. Why should you learn this when your billing rate is $300+ per hour? There will be times when you are working in the wee hours and you will need to send a fax, scan, or make copies. Skills like this also impress partners since they may not know how to run the equipment and will be pleased with your ability to do anything it takes to get the job done.

When I was a second year associate, a buddy named Leif, who is now the managing partner at a major Chicago IP firm, developed what we dubbed, the "Leif Shift" for photocopying cases from reporters (yes, associates once had to copy from casebooks). He would move the book over after the first page was copied so that there was no unexposed unsightly black bar on the copy. This shows that Leif did not find copying below his status, and he also strove to be the best copier he could be. Leif has practiced his entire career with that above the call of duty attitude, on every task.

As with any team, it is always important to have strong, friendly relationships with your peers. Although you may be competing with each other for some things, e.g., choice assignments and eventual partnership, the vast majority of the time you will be comrades in arms with shared goals. Your aims are the same: client service, winning a case, closing a deal, sharing suffering, survival, and so on.

In the early 1990s, I worked with a junior associate who was a decent person, but had an attitude of superiority among her peers. I always attributed this to her lack of participation in any competitive team sports or group arts programs where she may have found team spirit and humility. She was also very attractive and a daddy's girl, accustomed to getting her way with the mostly male populated IP lawyers. Whatever the reason, although she was not disliked, no one was willing to go out of their way to help her. It may seem unfair, but she actually brought this on herself.

Here's an example of her off-putting attitude so you don't re-peat it. I will call her Cindy. Cindy asked me to cover her desk while on vacation for a week, something you need a teammate to do. As part of this, Cindy left me a stack of files she claimed needed immediate attention during that week. After she left, I reviewed the files and discovered that there were no deadlines or other due dates, but rather, Cindy had dumped a bunch of bor-ing, thankless tasks on me under the guise of vacation coverage. Needless to say, this did not sit well. I mentioned it to another junior associate who said Cindy had pulled the same stunt with him last vacation! She had a pattern of manipulating coworkers. Would you go out of the way to help her the next time?

When I was a second-year associate, we had a major appellate brief to file with the Seventh Circuit. Our client had won $65,000,000 at trial and the verdict was not surprisingly appealed. A slacker mid-level associate was in charge of all the procedural aspects of our appellee response brief, e.g., indexing, binding, record transmittal, service, copies, exhibits, and the like. He probably gerrymandered this assignment as a way to get out of doing any real legal work.

I had to cite check all the cases and write the first draft of an important legal argument for the appeal. Another junior associate had an equal burden, as did a junior partner. Needless to say, the team spent a lot of time on the appeal and much was at stake for the client, the firm, and our young careers.

Finally, after hundreds of hours, the due date arrived, and the brief was ready to file. The slacker mid-level associate and I wanted the satisfaction and security of filing the brief ourselves (pre-electronic filing, again). We walked to the U.S. Court of Appeals for the Seventh Circuit in downtown Chicago and smartly slapped the red, bound briefs on the clerk's counter. One of the crusty Chicago deputy clerks looked at the filing, thumbed through a few copies of the clean, red books, and asked, "Where is the jurisdictional statement. It's missing from the first page."

The slacker associate, white as a ghost at this point, stammered, "We're the appellee, we're relying on the appellant's statement." Nice try. Unfortunately, Fed. R. App. P. 28(b)(1) stated unequivocally that the appellee's brief must include a jurisdictional statement. What do you do? It's 4:00 p.m. on the day the brief is due in your multimillion dollar case; there's no way you can insert the statement and rebind the briefs in time. The mid-level associate was frozen with his jaw agape, probably thinking of how he could pin his error on someone else.

I asked the clerk simply, "What should we do?" I didn't bluster or make demands or yell, threaten or curse; that was the right move.

The clerk, obviously knowing what the case was about and seeing this mistake before, said, "Well son, you have two options. One, you could handwrite on the first pages that you do not contest jurisdiction, but for a such a huge case that might not look so good. Or if you came back at 8:00 tomorrow morning before we officially advance the clerk's RECEIVED date stamps to the next day, I will stamp the briefs with today's date, and they would be timely filed."

Neat trick, and one you cannot do now with e-filing. We spent the night rebinding the briefs, sheepishly knocked on the clerk's locked door at 8:00 the next morning, and gratefully accepted the previous day's date stamp on the papers. The mid-level associate received a nice reaming from the senior partner on the case, but it was a no harm, no foul situation. Had I treated the deputy clerk with contempt as a low level, underpaid, patronage hired, do-nothing instead of with respect, the result could have been devastating at worst, or incredibly embarrassing for the client and our team at best. The clerk had been around a long time and had undoubtedly seen this type of error before. The clerk's office too was a team player in the legal system.

While most legal staff at private firms are high quality, there are always some bad apples. Many firms have personnel whom I call fixtures. These are usually staff members who are entrenched in their jobs, exude negative energy, and are generally unpleasant. These folks often are assistant office managers, "hot potato" secretaries, lower level comp and benefits staff, after-hours document processors, and the like. They are the opposite of the can-do, go-getter associate that you want to be.

What's the best way to deal with fixtures early in your career? Avoid them as much as possible. When unavoidable, be polite and do not engage them in combat. Their negativity is like a tar pit—get too close and you're stuck. They are called fixtures for a reason; if you bang your head against a fixture, the result is a headache and nothing more.

A final word on what to do if you truly can't stand your co-workers and wouldn't socialize with them if they were the last people on earth? Look for a new job. Gone are the days when people gutted out miserable positions until retirement just for the pay. Recognize that you have options, and when the time is right, make the move. More about this later. Next, on to how to stand out from the crowd while still being a team player.

CHAPTER 11

SHINY HAPPY PEOPLE—PERSONALITY AND STANDING OUT

Successful lawyers need to have positive and optimistic personalities. Contrary to popular belief, very few total jerks succeed in big law firms; it is rare that an obnoxious or boring or obsequious associate is going to make it far.

Unfortunately, most law students have had little exposure to practicing lawyers except fictitious ones from *Law & Order* or John Grisham movies. Unlike popular depictions, most successful lawyers are not obnoxious jerks. Good lawyers turn up the heat when they need to, but the smooth slasher is the model of success in most cases. The smooth slasher is just as aggressive as Al Pacino's memorable character Arthur Kirkland from *In Justice for All* ("YOU'RE out of order! YOU'RE out of order! THE WHOLE TRIAL is out of order!"). But she doesn't scream or spit as much. Think Elle Woods in *Legally Blonde*.

The difference is one of style, not energy, dedication, or success. The truly great trial lawyers, Clarence Darrow, David Bois, Johnnie Cochran are and were smooth slashers, as were fictitious ones like Perry Mason and Atticus Fitch. Their intellect, preparedness, charm, and charisma achieved results. Great corporate lawyers are the same, but usually with a lower profile than trial attorneys. Being a smooth slasher means you always tell the truth, but as a judge friend says, "Not necessarily the entire truth." Screaming and blustering, truth bending and promise breaking does not close deals or win cases; strategy, thoughtfulness, and integrity do the job.

> ### Caren's Advice
>
> Remember to maintain your positive nature when accepting and working on assignments—all assignments. Whether you are on your 20th hour of work in a day or your 411th box of documents, smile and exclaim "all is well!" when asked. Partners and clients love lawyers with a can-do attitude. It sounds silly, but it is human nature. You want to work with people who enjoy what they do.

Jerks do not make it in firms, even individuals with good skills. Look at your school or new firm; who are the leaders and who are recognized as the best students and lawyers? They are usually decent people. The really obnoxious attorneys may have a place as hatchet men or women, but they usually exist on the fringes and in the shadows.

Not being a jerk doesn't mean being boring. You must have a strong, positive personality to succeed. You should not go against your nature, and don't be afraid to show flare, eccentricities (if interesting and benign), interests, and hobbies. Don't be a bump on the log or too serious and grim.

Before the existence of e-mail, one of the serious, bordering-on-grim junior associates at my patent firm sent a written memo to all personnel stating that someone had taken his special coffee mug and he wanted it back. It was not a funny memo or self-deprecating; he was serious! The other associates and even the partners ribbed him for *years* about it. Don't be known as a grim, humorless tool.

The other personality no one likes is the sycophant. This situation is a little trickier since most managers expect *some* degree of deference, ambition, and commitment from the associates, but they don't want a total ass-kisser. This is where you need to see what works with particular partners and senior attorneys and react accordingly. The older founding partner may command and demand respect, or she may eschew it, not wanting to appear crotchety or antiquated. On the other hand, the junior partner may feel she now deserves recognition of her office, or she may want to still be "one of the gang," showing everyone that nothing has changed. You will need to judge the situation and adapt to different styles and demands. This may not be so easy, but if you stick with your fundamental personality traits, and simply modify but not radically alter them, you should be OK.

Your personality is your best ally. You made it this far, and you can thrive at the firm with the right planning. Your personality and skills will allow you to market yourself to your coworkers and to the outside world. Next are some basic considerations in the very complex area of law firm marketing.

CHAPTER 12

GO AHEAD AND SHOUT—DIAL "M" FOR MARKETING

Gone are the days when law firms won't market their services. Even the most prestigious, white shoe bastions engage in marketing. Marketing is not *advertising*, however. That would be unseemly for a big firm. Some lawyers advertise on late-night TV and on the cover of phone books; big law firms don't advertise, they market.

What is your role as a junior associate in marketing and promoting the firm and your practice? Most firms will not want junior associates to attract or aggressively seek new clients. In fact, this is often discouraged since you are expected to spend the first years of your practice learning the law and servicing firm clients. That is not to say that if you landed all of the anti-trust litigation for Microsoft that partners would be mad, but your primary place as a junior associate is to perform outstanding and voluminous work for existing firm clients.

This being said, you should expect to hear lines like, "As a junior associate, your best marketing is to produce high quality work," or some variation on the theme. Correct. As a junior associate your best bet is to instill confidence in senior lawyers and clients by providing timely, quality legal services. You will also hear the adage, "The best source of new clients is existing clients."

This relates directly to point one. The firm's existing client base generates many new client opportunities through expansion of the representation, referrals, spin-offs, acquisitions, and personnel changes. The deputy general counsel trades up to be GC at FleeceCo. Loved your work; gives you a call.

While most firms do not expect or want their junior associates to market, you will hear mention of "business development potential." What does it mean? Your biz dev potential will be measured chiefly by whether you can instill confidence in clients as a face person. A face person is not necessarily a glad handing, outgoing fraternity-rush-chairman type. A face person can even be bookish and shy. The key is the ability to instill confidence in clients and be service oriented. You can accomplish this through intelligence, drive, personality, attention to detail, super service, and more. You have to look for what the partners expect in a face person—this may vary from partner to partner—and project that image. If you are at a firm that values deep intellect, the Porsche, Italian suits, and Prada shoes may have to stay at home.

The partner in charge of Cooley's Colorado office, and its founding lawyer, is a terrific marketer, but not in the traditional sense. He isn't a glad hander who is at ease working the room at a cocktail party, engaging in self promotion, and other things you might expect from a rainmaker. Rather, he has an amazing intellect and a manner that puts clients at ease. He does engage in plenty of networking, but in a way that fits his personality, as a respected and valued senior counselor.

Another thing successful business generators will say is you never can predict when or how new work will arrive. You need to be out in the world, actively participating in activities you enjoy.

This is how to meet potential clients and referral sources. If you like basketball, play in an adult league or coach junior sports. Fantasy sports leagues can be good networking opportunities, if you do not actually play. If you are religious or spiritual, become active at your place of worship. Take art or cooking classes; do yoga. Be involved in local politics, the co-op board, or the HOA. And, of course, do lawyerly activities like write articles, teach, speak publicly, and write self-help books. Social media can also be an avenue for outreach and connections to your various communities.

In some ways, marketing is like dating: you can increase your chances by using a generalized, Johnny Appleseed[1] approach; or you can aim a laser beam at a few targets. Both have merit. You should try to scatter a lot of seeds *and* focus on a few good prospects. As a young lawyer, Johnny Appleseed's method may be preferred until you develop specific skills and get to know the community.

Marketing can be fun and blend into your life and practice. Try not to think of it as a thankless chore piled on top of your caseload. A key to marketing is to do an outstanding job at whatever you try.

Caren's Advice

Caren's Advice: Here are a few steps you can take now to market yourself for the future.

---

1. Johnny Appleseed was a real person according to many published sources. Born John Chapman on September 26, 1774, he sowed apple seeds throughout the Northwest frontier. He had a reputation for kindness to all.

1) Keep up with your classmates. Even if you do not have the opportunity to see them regularly, connect with them through Facebook, LinkedIn or other social networking sites. Some of your classmates may be referrals of work and possibly clients down the road.

2) Become exceptional at timekeeping and projects. The partners with whom you work and their clients will appreciate the effort, which will hopefully be rewarded with more interesting work.

3) Learn the "big picture" of the case and know more about the case documents than anyone else. Your ability to take ownership will be limited if you focus only on your narrow portion of the matter. The more you know, the more valuable you will become on the case.

4) If possible, meet the in-house counsel at your level when working on a case. Take advantage of any opportunity to work on-site with the client. Understanding the case from their perspective will provide an invaluable advantage. Also, the in-house folks at your level will likely be promoted one day there or at another corporation. Stay in touch with them.

Your first marketing is internal—to produce the best work possible. No one is perfect, though. What happens when you make the inevitable mistake?

Chapter 13

It's a Mistake!—Missteps and How to Avoid Them

Mistakes. We all make them and like sandworms, we all hate them; that's why pencils have erasers. Some are avoidable, others happen no matter how hard you try. Hopefully you don't think attending law school was a mistake, or buying this book. When I write of mistakes here, I do not mean character issues like lack of drive, intelligence, or dedication. I have to assume you are a motivated, hard-working, smart junior lawyer. The mistakes discussed, both macro and micro, occur in everyday work.

Probably the biggest overall mistake young lawyers make is a failure to instill confidence. If the senior lawyers and clients do not have confidence in your abilities, nothing else matters. You can give the best legal advice and be ignored, work the longest hours and be unappreciated, and be the most dedicated, yet be thought of as the fool. Lesser lawyers can and do succeed over those with better skills when they instill confidence and trust. Some of this is personality, but most is just plain attention to detail and communication—things that are easy to achieve.

There are some simple ways to instill confidence in partners, senior associates, and clients:

- Always bring a pen and legal pad to meetings and

take notes. A confidence-instilling habit is to have a pen or pencil on hand at all times: in your pocket, tucked behind your ear, wherever. The pen is the lawyer's sword, and having one handy shows you are ready.

- Keep your voice mail and e-mail messages and auto replies current when you leave the office and when you return. *Never* have a full mailbox that can't receive messages.

- Be reachable by cell phone or e-mail.

Caren's Advice

If you cannot be reached right away, always respond within twenty-four hours no matter where you are or what you are doing.

- Communicate with your colleagues when you are out of the office. Partners, senior lawyers, and clients understand that you will take vacations or medical leaves, but can't stand it when someone simply disappears. Better yet, send around a vacation memo with matters, status, and contact information.

- Proofread all written communications for spelling and grammar.

- Re-record voice mail messages. If you misspeak delete the message, don't ramble.

- Conform all numbering, outlining, tenses, wording, pagination, and the like in documents.

- Utilize but don't rely on the "find and replace" function when you use forms; always proofread to eliminate vestiges.
- Be sure that your communications are professional and concise.
- Be positive about yourself and your work and toward peers, superiors, and subordinates.
- Avoid asking silly questions in "all hands" e-mails.
- Be very careful when using "reply to all" in e-mail, or better yet, don't.
- Meet deadlines and communicate about status of cases and transactions.
- Submit all your written product in final form, even if it will be revised.
- Think about what else you can do on a case or a deal.
- Don't make excuses.

Some real-life career injuring, yet avoidable, mistakes:

- A junior associate misspells the capital of Canada and sends a letter under a partner's signature to a major academic client, actually having instructed the partner's secretary to sign the partner's name (the partner went ballistic).
- A senior associate sends an all-hands e-mail inquiring about a very fundamental legal issue in her field of expertise.
- At lunch, an associate disparages his firm and its partners not realizing that the managing partner is sitting in the next booth.

- An associate, knowing of a deadline for weeks, leaves the draft of a summary judgment brief on the partner's desk the day before it's due with numerous missing sections entitled "partner to complete."

- During a very serious SEC investigation an associate "disappears" on a long-planned vacation without notifying the partners.

- And my personal favorite: after news that a colleague was terminated, a junior associate goes on a bender, disparages the management in a drunken rant, and misses work for two days with a killer hangover.

What is the theme underlying these situations and many, many more? They constitute self-inflicted wounds and are not the result of overbearing partners or lack of intellectual firepower and work ethic. These are scenarios that can dog an associate's career forever. During the partnership vote, someone will ask, "Isn't she the half-wit who sent around that idiotic all hands e-mail?"

You can't avoid all mistakes, but can traverse the really silly ones. Avoiding the obvious pitfalls will help you instill confidence and will advance your career.

What if you do make a mistake in your written work? TAKE RESPONSIBILITY. This applies to every other mistake you might make as well. The buck stops with you, not with your secretary, the word-processing pool, the copy center, another associate, or whoever else touched the document. As Henry Ford II admonished after crashing a car that was not a Ford in the company of a beautiful woman who was not his wife: "Never explain." Live by the Japanese business adage: fix the problem not the blame.

If a document has typos that you did not catch, simply say, "I take full responsibility. It should not have happened, and it won't happen again." And it better not.

The partner or client will appreciate your candor and sense of responsibility. Even if you made the change and your secretary forgot to type it, it is still *your* problem. You compound the error by complaining, "My stupid secretary can't make even a simple change!" Now you are not only sloppy, you also do not take responsibility and can't manage your staff. In this situation, YOU should have proofread the changes and YOU bear the responsibility. In the privacy of your office, you can constructively critique your secretary. Do not dress her down in the corridor; that will only be embarrassing and build resentment.

If a typo in a document needs correcting because it is substantive, perhaps an incorrect share price or exercise date, take responsibility and fix the problem immediately. Do not hope the error will slide by. Tell the partner or senior lawyer and with approval send out a corrected version, including a short explanation that you caught a typo and the earlier document should be discarded. Simple as that. Don't make a big deal with a lengthy explanation and a demand to return the earlier version—just play it cool.

If you filed a document that needs correcting with the court or the government, after you discuss the situation with a senior attorney, the best approach is usually to simply file and serve a corrected document. You can call it an "Amended" or "Corrected" version. This situation has happened to all lawyers at some point in their careers. It's embarrassing and shouldn't occur, but it does. Your colleagues and adversaries will understand if you handle the situation promptly, with poise and class, and if you don't repeat the mistake.

The worst thing you can do is to hide a mistake you know needs correcting. In deals and litigation, your opposing counsel, the government, the court, the client, or a myriad of others WILL inevitably discover the error. The cover-up is always worse than the crime, so don't try to bury the problem—take responsibility and fix it.

Caren's Advice

Every partner I know, over 3000 of them, has made a mistake such as this in their career. You will too. It is OK and correctable in most instances. The faster and more upfront you are in dealing with it, the better the chance you have to fix it before it is insurmountable.

Avoiding mistakes will help your progress over the years. As you mature in the firm, your salary and bonus will advance as well. Next are some observations about the numerous big firm compensation systems.

CHAPTER 14

MONEY, SO THEY SAY, IS THE ROOT OF ALL EVIL TODAY—HOW NOT TO SUCCUMB

You would think that the compensation structure would be about the easiest thing to grasp at your firm. Actually, there are many nuances and compensation is a way that firm management can communicate to associates. It is not healthy to be hung up on money. Most associates and partners are highly compensated and "keeping score" can detract from more important issues. However, you do need to know some basics about how your firm comps its associates in order to understand any unspoken messages.

> ### Caren's Advice
>
> Salaries and overall compensation systems in law firms are a moving target in the current marketplace. Do not be surprised if you accept an offer with a firm that employs a lockstep system to find out only months later that it has moved to a merit-based system.

Most big firms have two basic associate pay structures: (1) lockstep and (2) variable/merit. Lockstep firms pay each associate in the same class the exact same *base* salary. So let's say that every second year receives a base of $150,000, every third year, $180,000, and so on, no matter what. There are some typical modifications to the lockstep system that set different base salaries for different locations, e.g., the base scale in the New York City office is higher than that in the Atlanta office. These firms still fall into the lockstep category. Lockstep firms differentiate associate compensation with year-end bonuses. More on this later.

The other system pays associates in the same class year (after the first year) different base pay levels according to associate reviews, practice groups, productivity, and other factors. Thus, the star of the class will earn a higher base than the average or laggard; associates are often force-ranked numerically in this type of system. Associates in high-margin practices like M&A could earn a higher base than those in a commodity practice like insurance defense. In effect, the firms with differentiated base salaries reward and communicate to associates using the monthly paycheck instead of, or in addition to, the annual bonus that lockstep firms use. The variable system can be very effective at communicating associate value and assumes that associates will share notes about their pay.

Lockstep firms use the year-end bonus to achieve a similar result as the variable system. The bonuses are meted out using a combination of associate seniority, performance reviews, productivity (billable hours), and other factors. The management typically sets a bonus pool for all associates based on profits and then divvies up the money. For instance, the average fifth year is slotted for a $30,000 bonus. This amount is raised or lowered based on the associate's performance reviews, geography, and productivity. Thus, a strong performing fifth year with high billable hours in New York City may receive $40,000, while an identically evaluated fifth year with lower hours in Atlanta might receive only $30,000. The class laggard may be at $20,000.

Because most junior associate bonuses are compressed, the bonus figures communicate more information as associates advance. Thus, a weak performing mid or senior associate may receive a very small bonus, or even none at all, and there will be a wide gap between the laggard and the star. The junior associate bonuses are more tightly grouped, with distinctions based on extraordinary hours ("combat pay") more than on performance reviews. Thus, a junior class laggard may only see a small deviation from the average.

Why does this matter? It is important for you to understand the firm's bonus system so you can hear the review message tacitly stated by the bonus and have data points to maximize your comp, if you choose. Most firms have an absolute hours cutoff for associates to receive a bonus at all and will have reductions or increases based on attaining certain billable hours levels. It is in your best interest to know these tranches and know where you stand.

One poor sap I knew missed the next bonus level, and missed out on a few grand, by falling twenty billable hours shy of the mark for the year. Some firms don't credit pro bono or internal firm billings for bonus calculation. You need to know these quirks, too. It is usually OK to ask a friendly partner how the system generally works. But be careful not to appear greedy or obsessed with your pay.

> ### Caren's Advice
>
> You can always ask the recruiter too; he will be well-versed on how the firm's compensation system works.

External factors matter, too. If the firm has a steady or more profitable year than the last, since you are more senior, you should expect a bigger bonus assuming your billables are comparable. Then, if your bonus is about the same or less than the prior year, you need to recognize that the firm is likely sending you a negative message. In contrast, if you receive a huge bump that isn't attributable to extraordinary hours, you may assume that the firm thinks you are ahead of your peers. Some firms want high levels of deviation between each associate's bonus; others will try to smooth out the rough edges and make things level. It is important that you focus on your firm's system and what is being communicated through these actions.

It is far too easy to become obsessed with compensation. The key to a long and fruitful career is whether you are happy and fairly compensated over time. Bear in mind that a focus on minor salary deviation can be quite destructive and can lead to constant disappointment.

> ### Caren's Advice
>
> Speaking of disappointment, a quick note about loans. Pay them off soon. Why you ask? Because, in an ideal world, you will love BigLaw and stay forever. But what if you don't? Pay off your debt now, so you can take that low-paying, yet stimulating public interest job you are so passionate about (in the future).

Be aware of the message the firm quietly sends with comp; direct performance messages are discussed next.

Caren's Advice

The compensation system in law firms sounds complex, but it's actually fairly simple: do quality work, work hard, and you will be compensated fairly. That's my experience.

CHAPTER 15

WHEN TO HOLD 'EM, WHEN TO FOLD 'EM—GRACEFUL EXITS

If you have done your research, had choices, and hopefully summered at a law firm or two, your job success should not be a gamble. Professional poker players will tell you that luck has very little to do with winning a hand—it's knowing the odds, how to play, and how to bet. Big law firms are funny creatures, not like corporations or other professional service firms. For example, in most companies there is a clear chain of command, an org chart, and everyone knows her place in the hierarchy. In contrast at big law firms, the chain of command is dynamic, and the reporting lines are unclear.

Also, most companies have regular performance reviews of all personnel where direct and systematic evaluations are given by managers. Law firms, instead, often have an irregular or incomplete review process at times with little meaningful feedback. The comments are sometimes indirect and unclear for most associates. The few superstars probably know their place, as do the few who are simply incompetent. The vast swath in the middle have to read the tea leaves to determine where they stand.

My favorite associate review story comes from when I worked at a patent law firm early in my career. This is pre-Internet, pre-e-mail, and pre-bulletin boards and chat rooms. We were kept in the dark about everything. Year ends came and went. Routinely, no one received reviews. The junior associates were worried since the country was in the recession of the early nineties, and there was uncertainty and "layoffs" at some firms (of course, back then layoffs were stealthy, in the guise of performance terminations; no firm ever formally acknowledged or announced a layoff).

Everything seemed normal at the patent firm—there was work to do, we received regular paychecks, and there were no big changes in firm policy. Finally, the lack of review feedback drove the bravest of our ranks (not me) to ask a senior partner when the associates would receive annual reviews. The partner replied crossly, "You get your paycheck every two weeks, right? What more feedback do you need?" That summed it up in his mind. If you received assignments and a paycheck, that was enough of a review. Presumably, if your building pass is revoked, office packed in boxes, and you find a COBRA letter in your mailbox, that's the end.

Caren's Advice

If you are not receiving feedback routinely, ask for it. It is your career and your responsibility to take the initiative to fully understand where you stand in comparison to your peers.

Even when firms think an associate is not working out, managers are often not clear with their communications. Lawyers are typically poor managers and avoid difficult personnel issues. What are the code words that should cause a resume update? Here are some of the favorites I have heard over the years:

- "You should think about whether this is really the type of practice that suits you." Translation: You are not smart enough/hard working enough/dedicated enough/skilled enough for our practice.

- "Private practice at a big firm is really hard and not for everyone." Translation: You are not cutting it in private practice, try the not-for-profit sector.

- "You're such a nice person, maybe litigation is not your calling." Translation: You are a pushover.

- "You're such a nice person, maybe corporate law is not your calling." Translation: You are a pushover.

- "The partners are worried that you are falling behind your peers." Translation: You are not as smart/hard working/dedicated/skilled as your peers.

- "One of our clients is looking for an in-house lawyer; you may be interested." Translation: We would like you to leave but will help you find a soft landing where you will send us work.

- "Maybe you would be happier in a public interest or government practice." Translation: You are not cutting it in private practice, and we don't want to foist you on a client.

- "We are concerned about your hours." Translation: Either you are not hard working and dedicated or the partners don't have confidence enough to give you work or the ship is sinking.

- "We want to do everything to help you succeed." Translation: You are unable to cut it on your own.

- "You should consider taking a legal writing course." (Worse the more senior you are.) Translation: You are a poor writer, an important skill in most practices.

- "Have you ever considered business school?" Translation: You don't seem to be cutting it.

- "You seem like such a hard worker, but the partners have to write off a lot of your time." Translation: You are either padding your hours or are horribly inefficient.

- "You have to work on your ability to instill confidence in partners and clients." Translation: You don't pass the sleep-at-night test.

- "You need to pay more attention to detail." Translation: You are careless and sloppy.

- "Maybe you would be happier doing [insert legal practice that firm does not have]." Translation: We would rather you practiced elsewhere.

. . . and my all-time favorite:

- "We don't really have the work at this office that best suits you. Have you ever considered a transfer to our [far away and undesirably located] office?" Translation: Speaks for itself.

Just as all things change over time, associates' positions and value in the firm can shift from year to year. A star first year, like a sprinter, may not advance or have what it takes for the marathon of practice. A plodder's value may finally be noticed at year four or five. The influence of specialty groups within a firm waxes and wanes, along with the fortunes of their constituent attorneys. The power and motivation of partners also ebbs and flows through time. A powerful partner can slide out of favor during the span of your still-young career.

How do you weather the test of time? Plenty of self-help books on career development and preservation, usually with clever titles, are available. However, I do not intend this to be such a book. As an associate, there are things you need to know and need to do. The preceding chapters hopefully will help you along the way.

What if it doesn't seem to be working out? How do you even find out this important fact?

The main indicator of how you are doing in the firm is whether you are staffed on the best assignments and receive a constant flow of work. (This assumes the firm is doing well.) The best litmus test that indicates an associate or even a partner is not long for the firm is a sustained decrease in billable hours. This means that the lawyer is either not seeking or being sought after for assignments—a death knell.

If you find that cherry assignments are going elsewhere and you are not receiving new, available projects, this is a very bad sign. Actions speak louder than words.

Caren's Advice

And if your firm has a work assignment system, don't assume it is broken because you are not getting good work. Associates who are strong will continue to get good work if it exists. Associates who are not performing well will get little, if any, work. If this is

> you, find out why and fast. If you have fallen out of favor, do everything possible to fix the issues and get new projects to prove your value right away.

What are the code words law firms use to give difficult performance messages to associates? The first thing to remember is that absent extreme circumstances and layoffs, law firms rarely "fire" underperforming associates. Management tells them things aren't working out and it's time to move on. The firm may give a deadline immediately or may wait to see what happens. Why the kid-glove treatment? There are probably three reasons.

The first is historical. Absence malfeasance, big law firms typically did not fire associates; it simply was not professional and was not done. Those days are gone, of course, but the vestige of this professionalism remains at most places.

The next reason is that law firms consider all former firm attorneys, sometimes quaintly called "alumni," as potential clients or referral sources. Even though the associate did not work out at the firm, she might end up in a position to refer business or purchase legal services from the firm. The firm might actively try to place the associate in a client's law department for a soft landing.

Finally, in this day and age, there is always the fear of a lawsuit and/or bad press. Most everyone can cobble together some sort of employment claim. It is easier for associates in protected classes, and almost everyone these days (even your under 40—Anglo Saxon—protestant—straight—U.S. born—male) may have some colorable claim, reverse discrimination, sexual harassment, whistle blower, hostile work environment, whatever. The law firm will obviously fear cases that might have merit, but firms want to avoid even frivolous cases because of adverse PR and the remote chance of success. This makes business sense, especially when you consider the other reasons for gentle handling of performance issues. Also, firms are afraid of having associates disclose firings on blog and Internet sites such as *Above the Law*. The more "prestigious" the firm, the more it is afraid of any bad press.

These days some associates play the system for all it's worth. I knew an associate who wasn't working out. Not a bad person, actually intelligent and well meaning. For a number of reasons, it just wasn't going to be a long-term relationship with his firm. The associate started to receive negative performance reviews. Suddenly, the associate's supervisor was abusive, and the associate complained to the department head. There is no cause of action for having a mean boss if he is mean to everyone, even if the allegation was proven true. Firms take these claims seriously, however, even when they are marginal at best.

If you find yourself in the unfortunate position of not fitting at your firm, try to exit as gracefully as possible. In the long run there is no benefit to a noisy withdrawal.

Caren's Advice

Some firms will help outplace you, including paying for a third-party outplacement expert to review your resume, research jobs, and hone your interviewing skills. Others will expect that you will find a job on your own. If you have ample time to find work, decide what you want to do, network, and make connections in that area. If all else fails, use a headhunter.

CHAPTER 16

IS THAT YOU BABY OR JUST A BRILLIANT DISGUISE?—CASE STUDIES

What follows are some general types of junior lawyers I have seen and lessons you can learn from them.

Type I—The Super-Nerd

I start with the super-nerd because this is one of the most common types of junior associates and might include some of us. Also, the super-nerd, although flawed, has most of the attributes needed to be a successful lawyer in a large practice. He just needs a little polish.

The super-nerd has stellar academic credentials, is intelligent, hard working, nice, and eager to please. He has never really faced any personal failures and believes that hard work and native intelligence can accomplish all tasks. This actually sounds pretty good, so what's the problem?

The issues for most super-nerds are two-fold. First, they usually do not understand the business of law. Second, they do not have the self-reflective skills necessary to identify shortcomings.

The first problem is the easiest for the super-nerd to fix. Knowing the economics of law firms is pretty easy. Once you see that big law firms sell billable hours at a higher price than it takes to produce them, everything falls into place. This means, implicitly, that the clients must see the value of the work and pay the bills. This means that the partners and other senior lawyers have to market themselves and the firm in order to attract clients. Junior lawyers are a part of this system and need to know it.

The second problem is interlinked with the first, but on an individual level. If the macro economics is operation of the law firm business model, the micro economics is the value added by the individual associate. Many super-nerds, either because of their background, prestigious schooling, or manner of thinking, have a much more Marxist philosophy than a capitalistic one. The reasoning goes: super-nerd is brilliant and works hard, ergo super-nerd should be successful.

But like the firm economics, there is more to success than being smart and hard working. There is service, a certain type of charisma, the interest and ability to sell (be it your position, your client, or your services). The super-nerd needs to take stock of himself, identity shortcomings, and make changes.

Jake is a super-nerd. He grew up in Westchester County, graduated from a Northeastern liberal arts college, then a top ten law school magna cum laude, and went on to a Supreme Court clerkship. He is brilliant but not savvy—Jake does not understand the business of a law firm or how to modulate his work to fit client needs. Every matter was a Supreme Court case to Jake. Jake started off receiving strong reviews, but then slipped when he could not advance his skills in relation to his peers. In the end, Jake accomplished great results on a very small range of cases, but was not staffed on matters that had a budget or that required speed and finesse. Jake's big problem is his inability to self-evaluate and refusal to take advice from others. Jake thought he was the smartest guy in the room who did not need any help. While he may have been accurate about intellect, Jake never overcome these problems and eventually left to a smaller practice. If you see aspects of Jake in yourself, spend some time on self-reflection and try to find a mentor at the firm who can channel your raw intellect into specific legal tasks. And most importantly—listen!

Type II—The Super Seller

The next type is the opposite of the super-nerd, this is the salesman or woman. This associate isn't the smartest, perhaps did not attend the best schools, but has a charm, charisma, and drive that advanced her this far. The super seller is a good personality within a large firm, so long as others perceive him to be a *smart* salesman.

This type gets along with everyone, make friends easily, and grows professional relationships quickly. The super seller will be fast out of the gate, but must remember that practice is not a sprint. So how does the super seller maintain herself for the long run?

The key is to either be smart or get smart. There are few better combinations than a smart, sales-oriented lawyer. Where she stumbles is in the third or fourth year when real skills need to shine through. The salesperson must grow the skills needed to be a superlative lawyer as well as a great seller. How can she do this?

Again, the key is self-reflection. The super seller must understand her shortcomings and address them. The problem of the salesman is often one of overconfidence—everyone loves me, how can I fail? This may be true for the first couple of years, but skill development really does matter in law firms. If you are not the strongest writer, take every chance to learn writing and participate in substantive projects. Mistakes and learning early in one's career are acceptable and encouraged; if you wait too long, avoiding substantive issues, your problems will eventually become too big to fix.

Maria is a super seller. She was a communication and kinesiology major at SMU. She is smart (enough), charismatic, and knows how to sell herself. Maria was staffed on great cases from the get-go and made a terrific first impression. The problem: Maria is just not intelligent, serious, and hard working enough to make it at a major firm. Once her charms wore thin, Maria lost the support of the senior lawyers and left the practice of law altogether. Last heard, she ran a yoga studio in the Bahamas. What if you are a Maria? You make a fantastic first impression, and your charm can take you far, but you must work hard, very hard. Know yourself and make up for perhaps a lack of book smarts with hard work and savvy. You have great assets and can succeed if you know your shortcomings.

Type III—The Do-Gooder

The do-gooder is an interesting personality. This is a lawyer who is really interested in public service and changing the world, but is at a big firm instead of the public sector or a not-for-profit. Although it seems incongruous, there are a significant percentage of do-gooders in private practice, and there is really no conflict in this so long as the do-gooder understands the business of law. Sometimes the do-gooder needs to pay off loans or sometimes there is the view that he can have it all, a big paycheck and a pro bono practice.

As mentioned in the super-nerd discussion, it is critical to understand law firm economics. Big law firms have large over-heads—associate salaries, nice offices, support staff—and it takes a certain number of billable and collectible hours to cover expenses. The do-gooder often does not understand that pro bono hours, while important for many reasons, do not contribute directly to the bottom line.

While firms should encourage pro bono, the key is the do-gooder must find a balance between pro bono work and billable hours. Even if your firm gives full billing credit for pro bono hours, this does not mean that month after month, year after year, you can amass huge amounts of pro bono time. Like every-thing, find a happy middle ground.

If you had an important pro bono case that absorbed hun-dreds of hours one year, the next year balance off your time with more billable work. If you know that a pro bono matter will heat up in the future, "bank" billable hours ahead of time to keep the right mix.

The thing to remember is that even though firms encourage pro bono and other forms of community service, they are still in business to cover expenses and make a profit. You chose a big firm verses a lower paying public sector job knowing this balance. You have to be able to live with the tradeoff.

Sam is a do-gooder. He has great credentials and is truly a brilliant junior lawyer. In his first year, Sam logged 1000 pro bono hours on a case. The partners said great job, but counseled that he must now balance pro bono time with billable work. The second and third years followed the same pattern. Finally, Sam would turn down billable projects and only take on pro bono work. Sam was let go for not developing the skills needed to succeed in private practice and for failure to find balance between billable and public service work. Sam landed on his feet and is now very successful, having learned a bit later in his career that firms have to pay the bills just like all businesses. Public service is invaluable for so many reasons, but you must find a balance. If you are a do-gooder, modulate your time so that you find a happy medium between public interest work and billable hours. After all, you are in private practice, and the management will expect results in exchange for pay higher than the public sector.

Type IV—The Nice Guy

The nice guy is the type of associate you would hope could survive the marathon. He is a genuinely kind person and has strong legal skills. The nice guy should not be confused with the do-gooder. He does not necessarily believe in causes, but rather strives to be a decent human being. The nice guy can succeed, but needs to sharpen his survival skills.

As mentioned in previous chapters, there is nothing wrong with being nice, and many great lawyers are decent people, not jerks. The nice guy needs to know, however, that life is not always as fair and kind hearted as he is; he must stake out and defend his own interests.

The nice guy might be too deferential when it comes to staffing on plum assignments, too soft on opposing counsel, and generally adrift in the law firm, lacking goals and vision. The nice guy can still be a kind person while defending himself and his clients. You are not a mean person simply because you want great work for top clients. Ambition and good nature are not mutually exclusive.

The key to success for the nice guy is to add a layer of competitiveness atop the core of good nature. This can be done without sacrificing the values the nice guy cherishes. If successful in having a fire in the belly while retaining a good heart, the nice guy can achieve a very successful and satisfying career.

Jaime is a nice guy. Throughout his associate years he sought out every opportunity to mentor junior lawyers and be the kind face of the firm. He was very skilled and made partner. Jaime has the shoulder that people cry on and gives very generous performance reviews. Jaime succeeded because he is nice, but also very skilled, hard working and knows the legal business. Jaime learned that you can be a good, supportive colleague and do what it takes to succeed. If you are a nice guy or gal, you can keep that attitude and be a great lawyer. If the rest of your skills are solid, there is no penalty for being kind.

Type V—The Go-Getter

Senior attorneys and clients love the go-getter. She has that upbeat, can-do attitude that shows loyalty and a strong work ethic. Like a Labrador Retriever, but smarter, the go-getter is an asset to the organization and a valued member of the team. Go-getters have enthusiasm, drive, and dedication, will log the hours and sweat the details of all transactions.

What is the potential problem with the go-getter? There are two main concerns. If addressed, the go-getter can be the perfect associate who advances through her career. The first concern is the go-getter is great at managing up (partners, clients), but can slip at managing down (staff) and working well with peers. The go-getter needs to realize that subordinates play a key role in the firm and need to be nurtured, just like senior attorneys.

Likewise, the go-getter cannot forget about peer relations. Many go-getters have infectiously upbeat personalities that lift the spirits of all associates. Some, however, gain ire and are seen as obsequious, self-promoters, or worse. The go-getter needs to be aware of this potential negative outlook and understand how peers might perceive her. If the go-getter shares credit and responsibility, makes friendships with peers, not just superiors, and participates in the formal and informal associate team building activities, she should do great.

Leilani is a go-getter. She never says no, takes on countless non-billable projects, and seems to live and breath for the firm. Leilani's problem is she has little balance in her personal life. As the years go by, Leilani finds it more and more difficult to keep up her pace. Eventually, Leilani has to take a break from practice. She returns as a part-time attorney with a set billable commitment. This suits Leilani's needs and forces her to say "no." Her firm recognizes Leilani's skills, and she is able to tailor-make a livable schedule. Senior attorneys love the go-getter, and it is easy to be charmed by the positive attention. If you recognize aspects of Leilani in yourself, make sure not to take on too much work and find time for yourself. It is fantastic to be busy, but you have to plan for the long run. If you are billing 2400 hours year after year, you will burn out. Leilani is not superwoman, and the hours will eventually take their toll. Find a balance, learn how to manage your time, and you can still be enthusiastic about your work.

Type VI—The Downer

The downer is in many ways opposite of the go-getter. Not opposite in the sense of lacking drive or work ethic, but opposite in terms of attitude. If the go-getter sees the glass has half full, the downer sees it as half empty and infected with flesh eating bacteria. The downer can be a real problem for the law firm and is often counseled out even if he has strong skills.

A downer personality is hard to change, but it can be done. With a new job, now is the time for a fresh start. A downer may never become a perky, sunny side up optimist, but he can temper a proclivity toward negativism.

The problem is no one really likes a downer—not managers, peers, or subordinates. Studies show that employees who are constantly negative become viewed negatively by managers. The negativity becomes a taint. Thus, if you think you are in this category, take time for some serious reflection. Once you realize there is an issue, you can embark on some self-improvement measures.

These can be very simple—just don't express negative opinions unless the issue is really serious. Try to be upbeat even if you might disagree with a course of action. Do not gossip about the firm, attorneys, or clients. Do not repeat rumors or obsess about possibly negative aspects of the firm or practice. Don't complain too much about hours, work, or finances. Don't share negative aspects of your personal life.

The downer can suck the life out of a practice group. This is the management challenge with downers—they can harm an entire area of practice. Since the downer can be such a serious concern, it is important that downers recognize their downerness, and take steps to improve.

Raj is a downer. He is pessimistic about everything, and this affects his ability to think strategically. It is hard for supervisors to give a review to Raj that reflects this problem. Raj is like Eeyore from *Winnie the Poo*, whereas the go-getter is Tigger. Raj needs to find a good deal of self-evaluation and wisdom to figure out his problem and take steps to solve it. In the end, Raj could be a great associate; even though he will never bounce down the halls, a small attitude change could do wonders.

Type VII—The Leader

The leader encompasses many of the positive traits of the go-getter and the salesman. She may also have the strong intellect of the super-nerd with a heart of gold like the do-gooder and some of the practical instincts of the downer, without the negativism. Obviously the leader is cherished in the firm and can have a brilliant future.

The leader knows her role, but takes charge. The leader is positive, yet realistic. She can be charming, but with intelligence to back it up. The leader does not want to fail, but is not afraid to assume new and difficult challenges. Above all, when senior lawyers talk about the leader, the main comments are maturity, poise, and skills beyond her years of practice.

How can you be the leader? Most leaders have innate personality traits that are hard to learn. If you have these skills, utilize them while at the same time developing the blocking and tackling needed in early practice development. If you do not have a leadership personality, you can work on confidence and team skills that will bolster strong basic practice skills.

In the end, not everyone can be the leader all the time. However, all associates can have leadership skills that will allow them to assume leadership roles when appropriate and take ownership of difficult matters. There will be many opportunities to shine if you look for them and are ready. The adage that luck favors the well prepared applies to potential leaders. If you have skills, confidence, and the respect of peers and managers, you will find leadership opportunities and they will find you.

MJ is a leader. She is a team player and is not afraid to take on critical roles. Importantly, MJ is accountable—the buck stops with her. As a junior associate, she leads by example. She has great skills managing up and down and has a bright future. MJ is one of those born leaders, captain of the soccer team, lead in school play, student council president. The key to MJ's success is that she knows that her past is also her prologue. MJ knew she has succeeded in other areas of her life, education, sports, student government, and then transferred that confidence to the law firm. It is very important that MJ, and associates like her, build on past success and not fear their new situations. You will be fearful of this new job, but look at your past success as prologue to a brilliant future.

Type VIII—The Chameleon

The chameleon is the most interesting and has the most potential of all associates. The chameleon is like the kid in high school who was not a part of any one clique, but was friends with everyone, a floater. Ferris Bueller is a chameleon. The chameleon is not two-faced or disingenuous, but actually has the many traits and plays different roles at different times.

One of my former partners and friends Wayne, an up-and-coming nationally known patent litigator, fits the chameleon model. When working with inventors and experts he is the super-nerd. When pitching clients he is a solid salesman. He teaches patent law at the local law schools, in part out of a desire to give back to the community. He is not a pushover, but can be a nice guy with trusted colleagues. The go-getter shines through with tireless litigation strategy, marketing, and mentoring of associates. He is a leader of subordinates, but also a good soldier to respected senior partners.

In sum, it is hard to fight the role that you naturally fall into, but, as always, self-awareness is key. You must understand your personality and take steps needed to smooth rough edges and add necessary skills. Saying simply "take me as I am" is not a good long-term strategy for success. Personality skills, just like academic and knowledge skills, can develop and change over time. Take the opportunity of a new career for self-assessment, goal setting, and appropriate change.

EPILOGUE

IN THE END IT DOES MATTER—THE LAWYER'S ROLE IN SOCIETY

Discourage litigation. Persuade your neighbors to compromise whenever you can. As a peacemaker the lawyer has superior opportunity of being a good [person]. There will still be business enough.

—**Abraham Lincoln,** Illinois lawyer, Sixteenth President of the United States.

This book is meant to be an informative guide to help your transition into practice. New lawyers should remember that there is more to the law than doing well; you also have to do good. You will have an opportunity to be a positive community leader and contribute time to good causes. I cannot encourage you enough to take an interest in your community and lend your time and skills to worthy causes. Volunteer for pro bono work, teach at a nearby school, assist with local and national projects, be a peacemaker and a good man or woman.

Many beginning lawyers have the mistaken impression that pro bono is only for litigators. This is entirely untrue. Litigation pro bono is very prominent, but transactional lawyers can actually help with litigation and even do a good job on trial work. There are also boatloads of groups that would welcome transactional pro bono skills. These can be estate planning, family law, consumer fraud, land use, licenses, contracts, employment; basically every nonprofit can benefit from free legal service. Seek them out. If your firm or local bar association does not have a program in place, start one!

Beside the obvious human value of pro bono and community service, they have many side benefits that can help with a successful career: networking, skills development, finding balance in life, recognition, marketing, advancement in an organization, and others. Find something that interests you—the environment, alumni activities, charities, neighborhood associations—and lend a strong hand.

Like other issues we discussed, your public service needs balance. Don't overdo it, and don't make commitments you can't keep. No doubt your firm will encourage pro bono service. Please do not be known by it alone, however. Public service can be the icing on a great private practice, but you can't make a cake out of just icing. Importantly, only participate in pro bono projects that interest you. If you take something on that you can't stand out of obligation, you will resent the work and the resentment will poison your experience. Find something you like—there are plenty of people and groups who could use your help.

I hope that this book has illustrated that you need to find balance in your life or you will not be in private practice for long. The myth of the type A, selfish, overbearing lawyer is simply not the norm in most high quality firms. Most successful lawyers are decent people. This may not seem accurate due to media stereotypes and misconceptions, but time will bear it out.

Your law career may seem like a marathon, but the miles will fly by if you enjoy the practice by seeking out opportunities and having balance in your life. In law as in life, the journey is more important than the destination. You want to look back at a career of accomplishment, but also of friendships and personal fulfillment. Have fun, work with enjoyable colleagues, seek out interesting projects, find balance in your life, be true to yourself and your days, years, and decades in private practice will amount to more than the sum of your paychecks.

NOTES

ABOUT THE AUTHOR
& EDITOR

Andrew Hartman

Andy Hartman is the Experiential Learning Program Director and Adjunct Professor of Law at the University of Colorado

School of Law. His duties include managing the law school's externship program, pro bono pledge, and moot court/mock trial competitions. Andy developed a very popular workshop class for extern students and combined the disparate competition program into a unified student managed body. From 2000 to 2009 Andy was a partner and head of the trademark, copyright, and advertising practice at Cooley LLP's Colorado office. Andy was chairman of the firm's junior associate evaluation committee for five years and was in charge of risk management issues for the Colorado office. Andy has been an adjunct professor of law at the University of Colorado, Boulder since 2001, teaching trademark, unfair competition and copyright law. He graduated from Georgetown University Law Center in 1989 with honors and the University of Michigan in 1986. Andy has been in large firm private practice his entire twenty-year legal career, being elected partner in a major Chicago law firm (Reed Smith f/k/a Sachnoff & Weaver) prior to partnership at Cooley. Andy maintains a highly selec-

tive private practice with the Boulder transactional firm of Gross Hartman LLC, which he founded. Andy has been an expert witness on intellectual property and statutory construction related matters, in addition to a popular speaker on IP topics.

Caren Ulrich Stacy

Caren Ulrich Stacy is the president of Lawyer Metrics, LLC. Caren has nearly twenty years of experience in lawyer recruitment, professional development, and diversity with law firms

across the country, including Arnold & Porter, Cooley Godward, Weil Gotshal & Manges, McGuireWoods, and Jenkens & Gilchrist. In the last two decades, she has facilitated the recruitment and integration of more than 2,200 new and lateral lawyers, and managed 1,500 training programs, 45 retreats and 30 mentoring programs. Caren was awarded the National Association of Legal Professionals (NALP) Mark of Distinction for Professional Development and Training in 2009 as a result of her vision, leadership, and innovation. She was also elected as a Fellow of the College of Law Practice Management in 2010 – an honor awarded to fewer than 200 individuals in the country. Caren is the author of several highly-regarded talent management books, including her newest book *For the Benefit of Your Clients: Effectively Selecting, Developing & Managing Your Lawyers.*

Caren is chair of NITA's Law Firm Advisory Committee and on the Executive Council for the Virginia Bar Association Law Practice Management Division. She has also served as chair and vice-chair of the NALP Attorney Development Committee, two terms on the board of directors for the Professional Development Consortium and as co-chair of The American Lawyer Chief Recruitment, Professional Development and Diversity Officers Conference. Caren is currently an adjunct professor for the Denver University Sturm College of Law Masters of Science in Legal Administration Program.